Advance Praise for *Hear Me, See Me*

"These straight-from-the-gut writings by incarcerated women will break your heart and put it back together again. Their words—powerful, poignant, inspiring, and unimaginably painful—are sure to become a classic in the growing body of prison literature. As the 'inside' writers change in the course of putting pen to paper, readers too will grow in empathy and outrage at their collective plights." —Sr. Helen Prejean, author, *Dead Man Walking*

"Everyone is imprisoned by something in life but most of us don't realize it. This book is about those who do. It takes the reader inside the prison system, yes, but more than that it takes us into the mind and hearts of women prisoners who are struggling to leave one world in order to become responsible parts of another one. It is about the journey through truth to wholeness. By all means, we should all read this book. Who knows? We may learn as much about ourselves here as we learn about them." —Joan Chittister, OSB, author, *The Way of the Cross: The Path to New Life*

"Gritty, graphic accounts of women struggling to find value in their mistakes, to honor their limitations, to master the self-limiting thoughts and negative emotions that keep every one of us bound. These women do the hard work that transformation demands: They take responsibility for their mistakes. They lay themselves at the feet of the Divine Compassion. They embrace their wounds and make them sacred. Then they write the lives they try to live." —Margaret Wolff, author, *In Sweet Company: Conversations with Extraordinary Women about Living the Spiritual Life*

"Incarcerated women's writings take us to places most of us have never been—the rooms where addicts live, the spaces where despair prevails. Yet, by writing about their lives, a glint of hope shines through. They want to improve their lives, they want to be seen and heard. By communicating with us and with one another, they are starting to connect with a better life." —Madeleine May Kunin, former governor of Vermont

"You cannot read these stories and hear these women's voices without feeling your heart open. It is only possible to remain closed, indifferent, and callous to those we think of as criminals or prisoners if we fail to hear them, listening not just from the head but also from the heart. These are radical, revolutionary voices because they dare us to do what society insists we must not: listen to and care about those who have been cast out and locked away. If we pause long enough with these voices and stories, we just might find the seeds of their liberation and our own." —Michelle Alexander, legal scholar and author, *The New Jim Crow: Mass Incarceration in the Age of Color-Blindness*

"*Hear Me, See Me* is a direct communication to us. Hearing incarcerated women's stories allows us to put judgment aside, and appreciate fully their histories, experiences and attitudes. *writinginsideVT* is a vital part of creating programs and avenues that help incarcerated women reset their lives and return to communities as productive citizens." —Andrew Pallito, Commissioner, Vermont Department of Corrections

"With compassion, empathy and respect, editors Redmond and Bartlett introduce us to the most invisible women in America: those incarcerated in our prisons. This poignant portrayal illuminates the complexity of their lives beyond their crimes. The power of their words inspires and pains us. This compelling account of life 'inside' needs to inform our gender-responsive policies and practices for imprisoned women going forward." —Stephanie S. Covington, Ph.D., Co-director, Center for Gender and Justice, La Jolla, CA

"In our work with children of incarcerated parents, we find the greatest barrier to maintaining and strengthening relationships with their mothers is the pervasive belief that these women have little to offer, and that children are better off without them. Through Redmond and Bartlett's work, we hear the truth—that by explaining and not excusing the behavior that led them to prison, and by sharing the insight they gain about themselves as women and as parents, they can give their children the unconditional and fully expressed love that all children need. This is a message that is important for their children's caregivers, and the judges, child welfare authorities, and prison officials who determine whether and how their relationships with their children will be sustained." —Elizabeth Gaynes, J.D., Executive Director, The Osborne Association, Bronx, NY

"Perhaps the greatest gift for a woman in prison is the power to leap through the bars by writing from her heart, to herself as well as to the free world. Her words and thoughts become her first taste of freedom. This book will help us understand and support these incarcerated women who made poor decisions, yet are good people growing in compassion and love through writing."—Sr. Elaine Roulet, founder, Children's Center at Bedford Hills Correctional Facility, New York

Hear Me, See Me

Hear Me, See Me

Incarcerated Women Write

Marybeth Christie Redmond
and Sarah W. Bartlett, Editors

ORBIS BOOKS

Maryknoll, New York 10545

Founded in 1970, Orbis Books endeavors to publish works that enlighten the mind, nourish the spirit, and challenge the conscience. The publishing arm of the Maryknoll Fathers and Brothers, Orbis seeks to explore the global dimensions of the Christian faith and mission, to invite dialogue with diverse cultures and religious traditions, and to serve the cause of reconciliation and peace. The books published reflect the views of their authors and do not represent the official position of the Maryknoll Society. To learn more about Maryknoll and Orbis Books, please visit our website at www.maryknollsociety.org.

Library of Congress Cataloging-in-Publication

Hear me, see me : incarcerated women write / Marybeth Christie Redmond and Sarah W. Bartlett, editors.
     pages cm
     ISBN 978–1–62698–039–6 (pbk.)
     1. American literature—Women authors. 2. Prisoners' writings, American—Vermont. 3. Women prisoners—Literary collections. 4. Women prisoners—Vermont. I. Redmond, Marybeth Christie, editor of compilation.
     PS508.P7H43 2013
     810.8'09287086927—dc23

2013005203

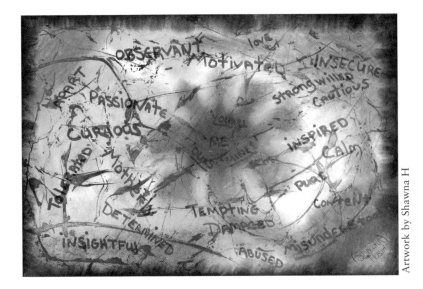

Artwork by Shawna H

Survivor

I am the flower; the black border, my addiction. It surrounds me with no space to get out. It's something I will have to live with the rest of my life. The words surrounding me are what my addiction made me out to be. I've been through a lot over the years and learned a lot from my struggles.

I have swum in the blue ocean of temptation, pulled myself out, and still face that ocean everyday. I've played with red fire, been burned many times; I still put myself out there knowing the risks, but I learn from them. The green represents my children, split because incarceration and rehabilitation tore us apart at different stages of their lives.

After months of struggling emotionally, blaming myself for many things my addiction has done to my life, I have finally seen my potential and am headed toward recovery. My children won't suffer forever. I keep them involved, helping them to understand me and how these past broken months made us much stronger. It's not their fault.

My past abuse (brown) led up to my addictions. I've been violated in many ways—and not yet completely healed. It's small because I no longer let my past control me. I no longer hide like a coward behind drugs and codependency. I've just barely started coming forward about the abuse. I didn't want it a part of my life. Little did I know it engulfed me and controlled me for the longest time. NO MORE. I am now in the process of healing, so that I'm able to speak openly of it without breaking down and becoming either emotional or angry or resentful. My work is still in progress. My addiction is forever. I can move on from this with the help of all around me who care enough to listen and I trust enough to talk to. I will always be me, but grow stronger everyday. I am a survivor.

SHAWNA H

Contents

Introduction

It is Thursday evening inside the only women's prison in Vermont. We facilitators, Sarah and Marybeth, sandwich together mismatched tables and chairs in a windowless room deep within the caverns of the Chittenden Regional Correctional Facility in South Burlington. This hodgepodge of furniture forms our weekly writing circle—more a haphazard oval than a circle.

A festive turquoise cloth and woven straw basket decorate the center, bringing a flash of color and beauty into this starkest of environments. The open basket symbolizes a receiving container to hold all of our words, no matter their subject or intensity. Relaxing Windham Hill–type music pulses throughout the room in contrast to the slamming metal doors and officers' crackling radios in the corridors beyond. White loose-leaf paper and Bic pens adorn the tables alongside the evening's printed theme and agenda.

Women of all ages begin to enter in chatty clusters, converging from various units throughout the facility: House 1, Echo, Bravo, Delta, Foxtrot, and House 2. Most are dressed in sweats, tees, athletic socks, and flip flops, clutching crimson folders that overflow with their previous writings. One by one they sign in at the doorway so correctional officers can scan this sheet conveniently during the 7 p.m. headcount without interruption.

We settle the group by striking a Tibetan chime. Expectant faces turn to listen to the reading of an opening poem by a well-known contemporary poet. Scanning the now-silent circle to greet the twelve-to-eighteen incarcerated writers assembled, we notice that "Annie"[1] is back from the "hole." Isolation is the main sanction used

---

[1] Our standard practice is to identify writers by first and last initials in blog posts and anthologies for confidentiality and adherence to Victim Notification System requirements. However, for this book, most women currently inside asked to be identified by their first names, their desire to be seen and heard made very clear. A few preferred to remain anonymous. Many share the same initials, but are in fact different women.

for acting out in prison. This forty-something woman with a floral tattoo covering her right arm suffers significant mental health issues, which manifest in periodic outbursts and assaults of officers and inmates. Her group attendance has been checkered lately, as a result. But tonight we learn something that earns her heartfelt affirmation from us all. Annie writes, "My gratefulness for this writing group has grown. To miss it was as heartbreaking as I thought it would be. . . . I cried [in the hole] every time I knew it was Thursday." This very night Annie is present in the circle because she has advocated for herself, telling prison staff how important writing is to help her process intense negative emotions in a healthy manner. As a result, she is now cleared for writing and mental health groups even when housed in segregation, and she has negotiated a staff escort to get her there regularly.

Such an accommodation tells many stories in one. For *writinginsideVT* it signals the value imprisoned women place on the positive personal and communal experiences we nurture by our regular presence writing inside with them. For the Vermont Department of Corrections it attests to the gender-responsive approaches being utilized more regularly with female inmates under new leadership at the Chittenden Facility. And for the women themselves it exemplifies the impact that positive role models, respectful listening, and inner reflection through writing can have on resetting their life priorities going forward.

Vignettes similar to Annie's abound in our experience. In January 2010, when we first began writing inside with female inmates, then housed at Northwest State Correctional Facility in Swanton, Vermont, we received regular feedback that struck us to the core: "I came to this group and learned my words affect everyone. I never knew what it was like to really be heard, to be listened to." And "Today I forgot I was an inmate and was heard by others for the real person behind the rap sheet."

Not to be seen or heard by others is a deeply painful experience. All of us have known such moments of invisibility when we've shared our souls only to be ignored, misunderstood, or rejected outright. But what of a lifetime of essential invisibility to an entire society that distances us with labels such as *other, without value, irredeemable*? This kind of marginalization describes the recurring experience of many offenders as a result of arrest, conviction, imprisonment, and eventual release back into communities. It is not difficult to envision the soul-crushing implications of ensnarement within such a system.

A twenty-two-year-old inmate who has been in and out of the system since she was sixteen articulates this reality best:

> I am a criminal. A convicted felon. I will have to check off that little box on a job application forever. Each time I get out, I go back to the same town I came from, where everybody knows my name, my crime, that I'm an addict with mental health problems, living in the only halfway house in town—where everyone thinks I'm nothin'.

Could any of us imagine a more agonizing place to reside physically, let alone in heart and mind?

In some ways, justice-involved persons serve as the biblical lepers of today, contemporary untouchables cast aside by communities across the United States. Many remain disconnected from families, friends, and healthy networks the rest of us take for granted. They live on the periphery of society, struggling to survive, tending their own psychic wounds in isolation. No wonder nearly half of today's female (and male) inmates will return to prison's predictable structure and quasi community within three years, an environment where the basic human needs of food, shelter, and safety can be counted upon.[2] Most tragically, these women live cut off from their own voices and dreams, not believing they even have a right to them. By writing together and witnessing the life stories of these incarcerated women, we provide them with a sacred space in which to reconnect with their lost humanity.

At the same time, we recognize that these women have hurt and in some cases devastated peoples' lives—those known to them as well as innocent bystanders. Unlike other states with populous urban centers where mass incarceration abounds, going to jail in small-town Vermont implies that their crime is a serious one. Their varied felonies run the gamut: assault, drug dealing, drunk driving, child abuse, robbery, theft, embezzlement, forgery, and even murder.

---

[2] A Pew/Association of Correctional Administrators survey asked states to report three-year return-to-prison rates for all inmates released from corrections systems in 1999 and 2004. According to the survey results, 45.4 percent of people released from prison in 1999 and 43.3 percent of those sent home in 2004 were reincarcerated within three years, either for committing a new crime or for violating conditions governing their release. The Pew Center on the States, "State of Recidivism: The Revolving Door of America's Prisons" (April 2011).

We want to emphasize that *Hear Me, See Me: Incarcerated Women Write* seeks neither to minimize these women's wrongdoings nor to ignore the harm wreaked on their victims. Yet their transgressions represent just a sliver of the multidimensional people they are—human beings composed of both light and shadow, as we all are. In this volume we strive to hear, and therefore truly see, the real person behind the rap sheet and to peer courageously through the powerful vehicle of their own words at the crisscrossing forces that led these women to crime.

It is fair to say that not one of these imprisoned women hoped to become a criminal when she grew up. A woman's journey to crime is largely related to the unique issues she faces as a result of gender. Several decades of research confirm the pathways to criminal behavior.[3] Females are more likely than males to have experienced poverty and various forms of victimization prior to arrest. The latter include domestic violence, incest, rape, neglect, emotional/physical abandonment, loss or incarceration of a parent, substance abuse in the household, homelessness, and mental illness, to name but a few. A large proportion of these women commit crimes while under the influence of, or to support, a drug addiction.

The majority of women we work with refer to ongoing physical or sexual abuse in their lives.[4] Many become involved in robberies and drug dealing as unwitting accessories to boyfriends—abusive men well-established in engaging depressed women in criminal activities in return for perceived intimacy. We have heard tearful stories from our women writers who trusted male lovers or friends only to be left "holding the bag" when the police pulled up to the convenience store or busted the crack house. Other women come to realize that their partners are destructive influences and decide to flee these terrorizing relationships with no financial resources, job skills, or work experience, turning to crime as a way to keep impoverishment at bay.

Longstanding cycles of trauma and abuse coupled with drug use can produce a monumental level of psychosis. Indeed, mental health issues are nearly universal; med-cart lines are long and frequent throughout the day within a women's prison. Inmates

---

[3] Long-standing research by Kathleen Daly, professor of criminology and criminal justice at Griffith University, Brisbane, Australia, has identified a series of unique pathways that lead women to criminal behavior (1992).

[4] Fifty-two percent of females reported some kind of physical or sexual abuse prior to incarceration (National Institute of Corrections, 2012).

housed in the mental health unit decompensate regularly. Corrections departments tasked with ensuring the safety and security of prisoners (in order to protect the rest of us) find themselves dealing with disturbed prisoners, some of whom would be better served within a psychiatric facility. The immense failure of our nationwide mental health system has resulted in our jails and prisons becoming a catch-all for those with serious mental health needs.

In our culture women must overcome a greater stigma than men for "doing time," and the societal costs associated with even short-term incarcerations are significant. Prior to arrest many served as the sole caregivers of young children, while others were working toward reunification with sons and daughters removed from their care.[5] Our cultural norms assign mothers primary responsibility for providing structure, stability, and emotional nurturing at home; when they fail in these duties, they are judged more harshly than men. With so many of their partners already in the prison system, who is left to care for the children? No matter how poorly a woman performed as caregiver, her powerlessness to make decisions from "inside" on their behalf is agonizing. The maternal anguish of separation from children is palpable week to week in our writing circles, as women tape photos of their babies to their writing folders or linger after group to explain the milestones revealed in the pictures.

Finally, the U.S. correctional system itself remains a fundamentally militaristic institution designed in the nineteenth century to be punitive in nature. It does not meet incarcerated women's needs today. Largely focused on security, uniformity, and harm reduction, the current system fails to address the behavioral and social differences between female and male offenders. Proponents of gender-responsive programs and practices understand that fostering an environment of safety, dignity, and respect, where incarcerated women can maintain important relationships to children, family, friends, and community, is paramount to their successful reentries.[6]

Hear Me, See Me offers the raw and unvarnished voices of sixty imprisoned women who hail primarily from Vermont but might as well be from anywhere. Their words as originally written, candid

---

[5] Over 66,000 women incarcerated nationwide are mothers of minor children; the number of these children—roughly 147,000—has nearly doubled during the past two decades (Lauren E. Glaze and Laura M. Maruschak, 2010).

[6] Stephanie S. Covington and Barbara E. Bloom, Center for Gender and Justice, 2003.

and unedited, provide readers direct access to real and immediate worlds. Much of the prison writing that has been published through the years presents the polished works of a few gifted writers. The aim of *Hear Me, See Me* is quite otherwise. We strive to showcase the writings of the spectrum of imprisoned women: from the nearly illiterate woman struggling to pen a couple of sentences, to the college graduate who crafts a finished piece effortlessly; from the dyslexic woman stumbling to read back what she just wrote, to the wheelchair-bound grandmother who utilizes writing as a form of prayer. This volume shares their deep humanity without gloss—their writings of course—but more important, their emerging voices.

Our model for this work is Women Writing for (a) Change, a program that has been changing women's lives through the art of writing and creation of community since 1991. Established by Mary Pierce Brosmer, the structures and practices of this program create a community in which social skills and deep reflection are both valued and modeled, making it much more than a writing group.[7] It is an opportunity to practice and experience change. As facilitators, we write as vulnerable equals alongside the incarcerated women to build a strong sense of noncompetitive, nonjudgmental community. "What draws me to this group is the sense of belonging together on a creative level, a sense of camaraderie," wrote a woman new to the circle. Others begin to draw strength from one another: "I took from today's group a new vision regarding my crossroads, especially hearing my feelings and thoughts expressed through others' words validating me." Caring for our writing community shows up in other ways as well; for example, when a new corrections officer interrupts our group for a verbal headcount, the writer nearest the door will spring to her feet and point out the sign-in sheet, indicating without spoken word that our collective silence is to be honored.

The group's Twelve Circle Agreements—values for living, really—are articulated and internalized each time we meet. We quietly celebrate when longer-term writers flesh out an agreement's meaning for new group members. Without exception, their favorites include reverence for the circle as sacred; that all participants are equal; the expectation of respectful listening; the absence of competition and criticism; and the presumption of

---

[7] For more information, visit www.womenwriting.org or www.marypiercebrosmer.com.

good will on each woman's part. We have been held aside after a session and thanked "for coming to grow with us" and "for being real and transparent with us; not many folks who work with incarcerated are like that."

For women who come week after week and persist in a regular writing practice, their written feedback reflects deepening internal shifts. An inmate in her fifties penned, "Walls and layers of thick skin have been pumiced away, as the words I write slowly begin to soften my heart and open my mind to new ways to release the horrors I kept locked away for most of my life. This group is absolutely my saving grace." Another writer shared, "I am able to speak without critique, to clear my mind of the negativity I endure every day, and allow myself to lighten again." Our experience has reinforced research showing that expressive creativity stimulates positive self-esteem, focus, and healing.

When we first wrote inside at the Northwest Facility, with modest financial support from the Vermont Arts Council and National Endowment for the Arts, we experienced the many tough challenges associated with creating sustained programs "inside." Reverberating, slamming metal doors, unpredictability of meeting space, erratic inmate attendance, extensive prison protocols, periodic lockdowns, and just plain organizational chaos provided a moving obstacle course. Through trial and error we learned that there is no neat way to gather, predict, or process an inside group, no way to address one set of requests without alienating another. For example, one unit's availability would conflict with another's chow time; moved again, a meeting could mean simultaneous triple-booking of, say, outside yard time, a sexual violence support group, and our writing circle.

Over our first eighteen months, through consistency and perseverance, we built a trusted presence with nearly one hundred women inmates. When the women were relocated to the state's most populous Chittenden County in August 2011, *writinginsideVT* was one of the first outside programs to begin operation within days of their arrival. All told, we have written continuously for three-and-a-half years with more than 150 inmates. Mothers and daughters, sisters, and long-time acquaintances have graced our writing circles. So have federal inmates and out-of-state women, short-term detentioners, and those serving twenty- to thirty-year sentences. Since Vermont has only one correctional facility for women, all are housed under one roof regardless of where they may be in the system. At maximum this is 170 women. Ranging in age from twenty to nearly seventy, a handful of "veteran" writers have participated in *writinginsideVT* from the very first session or two. We have celebrated their releases, only to have several imprisoned again due to parole violations such as relapse, a lack of safe housing, or additional crimes. These women have returned to our writing community and been folded back into the circle seamlessly. As one reincarcerated woman wrote recently, "I missed you guys. Thanks for taking me back under your wing."

We believe that women come on Thursday evenings to experience one another honestly, to gain insight into themselves and their prison mates. Their exchange of words provides a healthy release for daily frustrations: "Tonight I let my emotions free. I feel embarrassed to cry, but in this group I am comfortable." They console each other when setbacks arise around sentencing outcomes, max-out dates, or developments at home. "It's been very helpful for me during this time with my brother's death," wrote one fiery thirty-something after railing against God and the unfairness of losing her only close relative. Another reflected, "It was a gift to be able to let people know what I'm going through; hearing others, knowing I'm not the only one in pain." Some have remarked that the writing circle has become a neutral zone where the animosity of unit dynamics is relinquished for a few hours. Their writings show how hungry marginalized women are for affirmation and opportunity and how self-expression has boosted esteem, understanding, and confidence.

Recently, we posted a writing about one woman's drug addiction and subsequent crime on our *writinginsideVT* blog. She wrote of the "marvelous error" (from the poem "Last Night As I Was Sleeping" by Antonio Machado) it has been to land in prison, providing her with necessary reflection and regrouping time: "Win or lose, there was no end until one day, as in Monopoly, my Chance Card came up—go to jail, directly to jail." Her brother commented the following week:

> A very interesting piece my sister wrote. Although I have not had direct communication with her since her "card" was pulled, my hope for her grows as I see an acceptance that had not existed even six months ago. I would like to thank you for posting this piece. And thanks for giving my sister a voice, and for helping me see that it is time to reach out to her once again.

While our blog was created to connect imprisoned women's words to the larger society and educate the public about incarceration issues, we did not anticipate the possibility that family reconciliation might result. Another hunger revealed—that of families to understand loved ones who have strayed.

There is hardly any experience more counter to prison life than that of a dozen-plus women gathered around tables, heads bent, sighing, pulling Kleenex intermittently to wipe streaming tears, and quietly writing their hearts out to themes and questions posed by the opening poem.[8] We've explored early memories and wisdom we'd pass on to our kids; guidance and healing from the natural world; sources of strength, courage, vulnerability, doubt, and trust; voice and silence. We've focused on patterns of behavior, self-acceptance, resistance to change, struggles with body image and language, who we've been, what we leave behind, who we want to become. We've written about important role models and their lack—grandparents we've adored who raised us, siblings we loved or were cruel to; major turning points, like getting our first period as girls or loving the wrong men; personal manifestos for healthier living without drugs, eating better, practicing patience. We've created our own fairy tales or myths, imagined superpowers we'd like to acquire, envisioned ourselves as animals and flowers. We've written to verbal prompts, poems, prayers, letters, visual images, objects from nature, photographs; created mandalas, string art, collage, postcards; and explored improvisation and public speaking.

It can be heart-stopping when these women put pen to page. Although we never inquire, horrific details inevitably emerge through their writing. We've heard about the terror of growing up with drug-addicted parents and praying for rescue, brutal beatings by boyfriends, sexual abuse by relatives, "love affairs" with various substances, and going to jail for the first time. We have smiled inwardly at their creative turns of phrase for the prison facility we write within, such as "Razor Wire Hotel" and "Ice Island." We have been moved by references to themselves as "a slightly cracked child of God" and their invocations to the Divine.

We organize the writings into published anthologies, from which they read twice a year to invited guests at a "read-around"

---

[8] Poems and epigraphs from contemporary poets and writers were utilized as springboards for each piece of writing in this collection. We have attributed an original author and/or his or her unique turn of phrase only in cases where a line or title was incorporated verbatim into a newly created piece.

inside the facility. Many cradle their bound books like newborn babes, proud of the sometimes gut-wrenching work that has gone into birthing new aspects of self. At one recent event a writer's voice choked with tears as she recited her words before a circle of fifty listeners. Without hesitation the inmate to her left calmly assumed that woman's anthology and continued delivering her words in a strong, compassionate voice. How inspiring that gesture of sisterhood was to witness!

At another reading event, when refreshments were offered, women scurried to the spread, groping for cookies. Some stuffed their clothes with two, five . . . contraband to take back to their units. Writer "Mimi" tried to interrupt the madness without success. Her light-blue eyes flashing both sadness and rage spilled into, "It was a classy night, something real and special; but *they ruined it* acting like typical inmates." Yet Mimi's reaction touched us to the depths, demonstrating her yearning for one dignified moment beyond this prison world, alongside her protectiveness on behalf of this sacred community she has helped to create.

Writing can empower voice and celebrate change. According to the women themselves, their mentors, families, other program providers, and caseworkers, our program is enhancing inmates' ability to articulate, address, and alter their understanding and priorities, and in the process, giving us insight into our own lives. To paraphrase writer Louise deSalvo, what they write is less important than who they become as they write. The chance to be seen, heard, and validated for who they really are is empowering in an otherwise punitive, restrictive environment, geared to stripping away individuality rather than acknowledging it.

At provider and caseworker meetings within the prison we hear accounts of inconsistent inmate attendance at events or classes, overt rudeness to program leaders, disrespect to one another, name calling, and open hostility. We can only say that such reports are foreign to our *writinginsideVT* experience. Perhaps we hold a higher bar; perhaps the practices of shared vulnerability and mutual respect elicit the best in each of the women, as we believe. Perhaps our clarity about boundaries creates genuine safety, making writing therapeutic even as it avoids being therapy. Or perhaps the chance to be heard, really heard without criticism, judgment, or negative consequence, emboldens them to envision a different, more effective way to function. Our intention is to awaken them to their potential beyond the limitations and confusion of prior poor choices and to help them envision a future that is healthy and productive.

We have been fortunate to obtain generous private funding that allows us to continue offering *writinginsideVT* to an ever-expanding group of incarcerated women and an additional anonymous gift to help make this book possible. We couldn't have grown our vision for this program without the stalwart and enthusiastic support of our fiscal agent and ongoing programming partner, Vermont Works for Women.[9] Nor could we function seamlessly and continuously without the many fine assistants we've trained who volunteer countless hours with us. Currently, we are planning outside programs as women leave "Ice Island" and return to home communities to rebuild their lives—one day, one word at a time.

Our group of dedicated writers, despite their day-to-day challenges—shifting residences, medical restrictions, not seeing their kids, lack of food choice, and other physical and emotional deprivations—shows up open-minded and open-hearted. They share willingly, they go deep, they leave having touched something that moves and speaks to us all. The shared rite of unveiling gives them courage; it is a kind of communion that brings reciprocal transformation to all who partake. Their frank accounts of being broken, admitting defeat, and celebrating small successes challenge each of us to live more openly with one another, to face and transmute the hard, shadowy places within our own souls. As writer-activist Terry Tempest Williams writes, "In a voiced community, we all flourish."[10]

While our outside lives couldn't be more different from the incarcerated women we write with, we can relate intimately to the inner struggles and demons many of these imprisoned women wrestle with, day to day, week to week. Despite our many opportunities, our own lives have brought struggles with depression, voicelessness, and experiences of otherness. We have known, in the course of our years, similar feelings of being trapped, of not knowing how to get beyond the limitations that surround us. In some regards the relationships we have with these women are more authentic than many of those in our "real" lives. Here there is nothing to hide, spin, varnish. Life is as it is, vulnerable and in process.

The writings that follow have been arranged in three distinct sections representing both the common arc of an engaged inmate moving through our program, and ideally, the prison system itself. The first section, "Experience," starts where a woman is when she begins writing inside or doing her time. Her background and

---

[9] For more information, visit www.vtworksforwomen.org.

[10] *When Women Were Birds: Fifty-Four Variations on Voice* (New York: Straus and Giroux, 2012), 119.

life story emerge, followed by an examination of destructive past choices. During "Reflection," her ongoing writing leads to insights and spiritual connections. Next steps may begin to take root in her heart and mind. Trust grows, bonding participants into community. In "Collective Insight" individual words are woven together into "found poems" reflecting how unique words merge to create a powerful communal voice that nourishes all. That's not to say an inside writer's path isn't full of relapses and false starts—those are numerous. Yet the sequential writings mirror a real-time journey of the emerging experience, reflection, and collective insight that we have witnessed repeatedly among the incarcerated women with whom we write regularly.

When a human being has lost everything and has been brought to her proverbial knees, there is nothing left to fake, hide, or protect. Those of us living beyond prison walls can learn much from such a humble stance. These incarcerated women's lives can challenge us to live more openly with one another, to transform our own guarded places, to break through daily procrastinations, to free ourselves of bitter resentments, to realize unlived aspects of self, and to speak our own truths to power. Just as these women work toward their potential by reclaiming lost parts of themselves, the larger society, in order to evolve to its fullest potential, must hear and receive the voices of its most marginalized members. As uncomfortable as that may be for some of us residing in mostly well-ordered worlds, this represents our dual work in *Hear Me, See Me: Incarcerated Women Write.*

Experience

This is where the arc of each woman's experience begins—background and history that women bring to prison and that send women to prison. Women write of the real challenges to body and spirit they have faced—stories frank and revelatory in their stark telling of addiction, abuse, betrayal. These are their roots, the ground from which these women spring for better and worse. In some, the first stirrings of self-awareness and regret emerge—writings that share self-portraits and awakening to the need to break the silences and cycles of a lifetime. Such emerging consciousness is the critical first step to becoming whole, to heal and move on with their lives. Taken together, these writings lay the foundation of the values and behaviors—or lack thereof—that led these women to incarceration. Their stories could be yours or mine, but for one circumstance here, one missing role model there, one poor decision that will haunt them forever.

Artwork by CV

The Story of Fairy Dust

Once upon a time there was a magical fairy that would fly above children in their sleep and drop dust over them to give them beautiful dreams. Just as stories go, when the children grew, the fairy dust wasn't as strong and slowly faded away with the fairy.

CV

Twisted Lies

With your bitter, twisted lies, I stay and await a
   darkness that's unknown.
We first met on a bright lit midway; you told me
   you'd take care of me.
That was your first lie.
You brought me to a crackhouse filled with every
   addict ever known.
Your second lie was you loved me, couldn't live
   without me.
You loved me so much you wanted to pass that love
   among all your friends.
When you said you couldn't live without me, that
   was a lie.
What you meant was, you'd kill me if I tried to
   leave.
Your third lie was you'd protect me
as the man grabbed me by my hair and dragged me
   to the outside shed.
He went on beating me with a 4'6" board and
   stomping my head in as you watched.
Your fourth lie was I'd always have a home.
The next day, I went to jail with two broken ribs,
   trauma to the head with $100 bail.
From there I never heard from you again
with your bitter, twisted lies.

FLIP

The Blue Tongue

Try living under the threat of the large blue tongue waiting to reach out and grab you from the bowels of hell. It's awful. It's torture. It also goes by other names—heroin, dope, chiva.

I hear it calling from way off, or maybe it's in my head. "Do it, you'll love it."

OK, one more time won't hurt. I feel so good . . . Soooooooooooooo happy.

> I'm tired—gotta lay down.
> I go to bed and wake up to the alarm ringing.
> Has been ringing for two hours.
> Oh, NO—I need to get up.
> Where is he?
> He didn't come to bed.
> The side he sleeps on
> is not even ruffled.
> Oh, well, can't be far.
> I get up.
> There he is sitting crooked
> on the sofa.
> His eyes are open, he's cold
> He's not moving, he's stiff.
> This is not happening, it can't be as I'm disposing
>   of the syringe left in front of him.
> He was great.
> I don't want anyone to know or to judge him.
> Call my kids, they'll know what to do.
> The blue tongue is calling again.
> OK, alright.
> I need to feel right.
> I'm angry, but should be sad.
> He promised he would never leave.
> He lied.
> I don't even know where the kerosene can is . . .
> Why would you do this to me?

I felt the tongue swallow me and carry me to the
very depth of hell for months.
I felt nothing.
I felt numb.
I've lost everything
or so I thought.
When I thought I could lose no more, I sat and
talked to a person that I had just met.
He listened.
He seemed to care.
He was kind.
I spilled my whole life story in an hour.
Pretty bad, huh.
I then began to feel kindness toward others.
I wanted to live.
Because of this act of kindness, I did not allow my-
self to remain a prisoner, a prisoner of my own
mind.
I was no longer a victim.
I am kind. I've broken from the clutches that held
me down.
I am no longer a victim.
I am a strong and whole woman.
One act of kindness is sometimes worth more than
a house of material things and jewels.
I look forward to each new day, to the morning
dew, the sunset, and the frogs chirping.
The blue tongue for me has gone away, trying to
carry others to the depth of something horrible.
Do not become its next victim.

Laura

The Seed

After eight long years and one very unhealthy relationship, I was not only back in New Jersey, I was home. I never realized, all those years I'd been away, just now much I missed it—my family, the salty-scented air, feeding seagulls my French fries, lounging for endless hours on the beach.

I was newly single, reunited with longtime friends, with the whole summer to enjoy. I spent nearly every day on the sand, followed by the stop at our local beach bar where I'd unwind from my long day of unwinding with a Blue Moon and slice of orange. Then I would go back to my friend's to shower, change and return to said bar to enjoy my night.

This was the best end to a four-year relationship I could ever imagine! I wanted to stay single forever . . . Then one night, he came along. Perhaps I'd had one too many drinks, or perhaps it was his charming persistence; but after hours of flattery and laughter, I took his number.

First date was easy, fun, exciting as all good first dates should be. The second was less so, but I figured anyone I could speak to for hours on end was worth a closer look. The third date didn't go so well; he disappeared. Things quickly went downhill. Then it came, the inevitable ball to be dropped—he used heroin "recreationally."

Guess what? I have come to learn that that would be like me breathing air "recreationally." I became, not the girl he would give anything to have a chance with . . . without his fix, I was the girl that was a waste of his time. Needless to say, we didn't last long. I was fortunate enough that I didn't allow him to bring me down.

But he planted a seed, one I wish never had been planted. And eventually that seed took root, grabbed hold of my soul and like the most powerful of weeds, strangled and killed any beauty that would grow. Good thing, long ago, my grandmother taught me how to garden.

Jill

What I'd Tell a Poem

I'd tell the story of a girl
who woke up hating the whole world
every day,
the way she looked so sad
with clouds blending the gray
in her eyes like the mist
in the night;
until one day
those clouds faded
into skies of fire
blazing and spitting out souls of the damned
condemned by silver bars
cold yet warmed by thoughts
engulfed in metal chains formed
into razor wire that is constantly piercing
her skin, until a drop
of blood falls to a splatter,
a grenade being plunged
into a sea of silence.

That's what I'd tell to a poem.

AT

Innocence Destroyed

I remember when I was somewhat naive. Not naive about me or my body. Just naive to the adult world . . . As a child, I was forced to be a part of the adult world. I had sex long before I ever started my first period.

I was selling crack before puberty took place. I never noticed my body or the transformation. My mind was grown long before my body. Baggy pants, long tees. I wanted to be like him. Being big never mattered and even though I envied the other girls I grew up with, I never wanted to be like them.

I know I had more to offer than a body and a smile. My mind was worth more than what I had between my legs. I learned the hard way. At fourteen I was an adult. I fucked like a grown woman and I paid bills like a grown woman. All my innocence stolen from me. I didn't see it that way then. It was what had to be done.

I stepped into that role, took the burdens away. Made sure we'd be OK. I had far more important things to feel awkward about than a period or a body part. Or some hormones. We had to eat, rent was due. I thought they'd respect me more if my femininity was hidden. I was a little girl naive to the man's world.

When I learned about power and sex, that's when things changed for me. When I stopped believing in love. And that a man could respect my mind. All he wanted was to disrespect my body. And I allowed it because it had no value to me.

My puberty was a transformation from innocent to guilty. My eyes were opened to the harshness of the world. Love don't love nobody, not even itself. My puberty was a transformation to a realist. No more dreams, just nightmares. No childish hopes, just pain and screams. A little girl gutted at her seams. A woman emerges. Cunning and ruthless, the product of her environment.

Childish innocence and immature dreams seem so far away. Puberty spent in prison. Her transformation into a woman took place behind the fence. What kind of woman did she hope to be?

Stacy

A Letter Never Sent

Where do I start? Well, let's see. I want to know why did you leave me as a little girl? Why weren't you there for me, Dad? You had a chance to be a father, but you never showed up that day at court, so they signed your rights away and gave me a new dad, my stepdad.

I know when I was growing up you tried to kidnap me twice; once in New York and once in Pennsylvania; but you didn't get very far. I wish I knew you. I wish things were different. There's so much I want to tell you, so many things you have missed in my life: me growing up, me with a drug problem, me with mental stuff that I probably get from you.

I have two kids, both boys; you have grandkids and don't even know them or me. I'm gonna get married this year.

Sometimes I'm so mad at you 'cause you weren't there like you should have been, I want to know why you left me behind. What did I do to you? I just want to know who is my real Dad. What's he like? I have only seen photos of you and me as a baby. I'm so mad at you, but it's like I'm not whole 'cause of you; and I need to fill that hole with something. I don't even know if you're alive or dead. I look at my own kids, and I hate that their fathers aren't around; 'cause I know how they're gonna feel growing up, and I don't want them to be like me.

TIFFANY W.

Death

The only one great thing is Death.
Pain, misery, regret are no more;
eternal darkness my final cover
safe, secure, alone. The only thing
I've come to know and trust—
total and utter darkness. A sense of security.
A wall where no one can get to me.
A place to make a fresh life.

In the darkest of the dark, I'M FREE!
Death. Weight lifted from shoulders.
A place to find peace, lost souls, God.
A beautiful new world of dreams
never actually seen. A new friend
who opens the doors.

So open up your eyes wide! Change now
and make right, so when you meet that darkness
you embrace it, your open heart filled with love.
Change now so that goodness embraces you back.

DEBI

Will I Ever Overcome This?

I'm scared, actually, terrified.
This way of life has molded me.
This is who I am:
no dreams, no ambitions,
no motivation, no responsibility.
How easy my life goes by.
My other love,
my first love,
the one I gave away—
her nose up to the window,
watching me drive away.
Crying for me (the only one
that can comfort her);
and I still drive away.

DG

You've Forgotten

Slowly she moves, searching her steps
toward the voice that calls her name
across the path of tangled barbs
to a worn stone door in concrete.

She hears the voice, her name again;
it's softer now. The door swings open
as she reaches for the wrought iron handle
revealing a child. "It is me," says the boy,
"your memories. All that is left
is the wind and myself. You've forgotten
the rest," he says; "you've
forgotten yourself."

MD

Pillows on My Bed

I have heaps of pillows across the top of my bed, so if I need to cry I can grab one and hide my face in the bitter shame of all the painful, hurtful memories of my so-called childhood. Days when I would sit and hope that my father would be home in time to see his little girl on her birthday, but know he was not able to be there for any of that fun time, 'cause he was out working to make a life for his family. I feel all the memories coming back, how I would say, "I hate you 'cause you missed my life; but at the same time, you were trying to make a life for me. Well, thanks for trying. Sorry I fucked your world and dreams up. I'm not that perfect."

But we have some good memories too. I wish I could remember them now. I do remember a time when we went to the lake as a family and had fun; or the time I had my first child, how you were so happy to have a grandson.

Belinda

Where I'm From

I am from the forsythia bush on the corner of our house, the one my mother planted, it bloomed bright yellow every year. I hated yellow.

I am from fudge and eyeglasses, Grandma's fudge so sweet and wonderful.

I am from perk-up and pipe down, we must not aggravate her, shhhhhh . . . quiet as a mouse, the lion is sleeping now, put on my happy face for all to see.

I am from He restoreth my soul, and my life, ever watching, always caring for those who cannot care anymore—my Beloved Protector.

I am spilling old pictures of days forever gone, all memories now.

I am to drift beneath my dream, for I am a forever dreamer of dreams.

I am those moments snapped before I budded, a leaf fall from the family tree, but whose family? Did I fall as a leaf in autumn or was I torn by the strong winds of morality? Gone just the same.

I am a sift of lost faces, so many—too much to count, always changing, here and gone.

I am from all these things.

NORAJEAN

Gilly Was a Gangster

Gilly, he was a gangster. The hardest, toughest dog I've ever met. He had the most beautiful green eyes I ever did see. He had long, light brown fur. He always stood with pride cuz, like I said, Gilly was a gangster.

He had a mean snarl and an even meaner shake. Gilly didn't care that he only reached your ankles. He was a gangster. He used to latch onto Bigs's lips, he never let go. Not till he drew blood. Gilly didn't care that he was a long-haired Chihuahua and Bigs, a pit bull. Bigs had weight and height on Gilly, but Gilly always stood his ground. You couldn't take Gilly anywhere. He was always ready for a fight, even ones he could never win. That's what made Gilly a gangster. Taking pride in himself. Never willing to accept defeat.

I remember my sister used to scream, "if your dog kills my dog, I'm gonna kill your dog." Gilly was always protective over me. If anyone got too loud or too close, Gilly was right there hanging onto their pant leg, shaking and snarling, 'til we intervened. I remember when I first got Gilly, my sister named him after a goldfish. He was tiny. He would nuzzle himself right on top of my head hidden under my hair. Me and Norm, we turned Gilly into a gangster. My mother, she used to get so angry. She'd yell at us, "He isn't a pit bull." But Gilly was a gangster.

Gilly got dog-napped. And held for ransom. That bitch said if we wanted him back, we'd have to pay $2,000. I was angry. My friend, he wouldn't let me go to hurt this woman.

STACY

Mother's Cure-all

My mother in the kitchen; can we all say "disaster"? I love her dearly but the woman took nothing from Julia Child or Betsy Ross, for that matter! Mom was and is a fabulous woman, in her own right. It's just that, try as she might, she's not a conventional-mom type. The woman can burn water. I think we all would have starved if my dad hadn't known how to make pancakes, sausage and eggs for supper.

I, never having gained culinary greatness, am not a conventional mom, either. My mom, unlike me, didn't bounce in nightclubs or ride Harleys; but she was different from other mothers. She likes to be busy mowing the grass, planting a garden (in her younger years), or helping gather and split wood for our woodstove. She was always hard at work and usually helping my dearly departed dad—an awesome man. He chose her to be a mother and wife and she was good at both jobs. If it's a bump on the knee that needs tending or a broken heart that needs mending—always go to my mom. She's got the cure-all of love.

ELAINA

Lil' Brother

Strong, tall and handsome
 he never sheds a tear
 but he'll break your face at random
 just to hide himself from fear

His love is easily given
 but impossible to keep
 unless of course you're blood
 and even then it don't come cheap

We grew up being taught
 love equals pain
 So when he loves you he knows not
 but to repeat it all again

Through each other we have tried
 to rise above our past
 We were children at a time
 when innocence couldn't last

Each one we have our pain
 secrets we won't give up
 but when I see him smile
 for me that is enough

I fear for him the most
 cuz his demons I know well
 He is my other half
 my champion through hell

I love my brother fiercely
 how much he'll never know
 cuz sometimes I have to love him
 from places he can't go

MARGARITA

Baby Sister

When I am always around my sister, she wants me to be ashamed; and when I'm not around my sister, I'm not ashamed. The reason my sister makes me feel ashamed is because her life is better than mine. But I love my baby sister.

JESS

$\backsim$

My Son, My Mirror

I see myself in his face, those deep green eyes—the mirror to our souls. I look at him with great love and affection. But sometimes not. I see me in my youth, rebellious, angry, sadness and pain. These eyes cry out from deep inside—HELP ME, SAVE ME, LOVE ME.

I want to embrace him, protect him from himself, from me. Mirrored images, we two. Our hearts laid bare for all to see, reflected in our eyes—together sharing the same dark, murky memories. Things we chased after, never quite grasping the brass ring.

I love those green eyes. I saw them change when our lives changed. If only I could go back in time, to when your smiles lit up your face, and danced and twinkled in your eyes. My son—my mirror. Look into my eyes and see that we are as one with those green eyes.

NORAJEAN

$\backsim$

Missing Piece

I was taken away from my mother at a very young age. I did a lot of traveling as I used to call it, from foster home to foster home, from residential to programs and back again to foster homes, where I'd always have to adjust all over again, meet new people. It was so hard always having to try and fit in and feel as if I was part of this new family, these strange people, neighborhoods and kids I had to call my family, my brothers and sisters, my home!

Until this lady came out of nowhere and asked for a visit with me. I went for a weekend and although I had never met her up until then, and I never knew of her or her family, for some reason with her I felt complete. With her family I felt I belonged. After a while, the truth was spoken and I was told that this lady was (is) my grandmother. Her family was my very own.

And at last I didn't have to try to fit in or adjust—I was just the missing piece to their puzzle, and for the first time I felt it was meant.

Today I'm a young woman and my grandmother raised me to be strong, smart and wise, independent, and cautious of who I allow into my circle. Because of her, I've managed to forgive my own mother for her mistakes and accept her for who she is. My grandmother taught me everything I know today. She rescued me from all of my sorrows and only proved to me that no matter where you are or what situation you're in, blood calls.

JOSEPHINE

Guardian Angel

I wish I could turn back time,
as I feel a hand touch mine . . .
I start to walk and
feel a motion moving with me.
It is my mother's soul letting me know
she's watching over, never left me.

She's my guardian angel, my everything.
I talk to her when times get tough
and I feel like I've had enough.
Mom's taught me never to give up;
always fight, because in the end
things will turn out right.
I may feel like turning left
when I should turn right,
so I listen to that someone I can't see
that's standing right next to you and me.

Yup that guardian angel is my mom
who I'll be forever glad to call mine.
I know she will wait for a lifetime
to see me again,
but until then she will guide me through.

JOELLEN

Thanks to You, Mom

Thanks to you, Mom, I learned to keep a wonderfully
    clean, outwardly inviting home.
And by doing so, I learned to mask the Dark Dungeon
    lurking inside, the House of Horrors.

Thanks to you, Mom, I learned the art of cooking
    wholesome, delicious well-balanced meals.
Creating the illusion you cared for and loved those
    you invited to the table.

Thanks to you, Mom, holiday traditions and decora-
    tions, a beautiful sight to see, so elegant.
And happy they appeared to be, for all of us, sur-
    rounding our home so beautifully.

Thanks to you, Mom, by watching you and observing
    others, a sense of stylish fashion was learned by me.

Thanks to you, Mom, I learned how to be alone,
amusing myself with sticks and stones.

Thanks to you, Mom, I birthed a world of fantasy
    and make-believe,
one where I always lived happily.

Thanks to you, Mom, I learned to suffer in silence,
to never reveal my world of violence.

Thanks to you, Mom, all the things you taught me
    will never be passed on,
the nightmare of you has finally gone.

Thanks to you, Mom, I learned my lessons well;
but I can't see why I would ever want to be like you
    and make my children's lives an absolute living hell.

NORAJEAN

Daddy's Letter

When I was twelve or thirteen years old, I was very emotional about not receiving a letter from my aunt when both my mom and my little sister received one. Why hadn't she written to me? I cried for hours and eventually cried myself to sleep.

A few days later, the hurt subsided and the pain controlled, I got the mail and—lo and behold!—there was a letter addressed to me!!! I immediately recognized the handwriting as that of my father. That burly, hard-working, self-educated man had sat down and written a letter to his eldest daughter because he saw she was in pain and feeling left out. It was a short letter. I have lost track of it in the years that have passed. But I will always remember the love that it showed just because he sent it to me; just because he, a man who never wrote letters to anyone else that I knew of, wrote a little note to tell his daughter how proud he was and how much he loved her.

When I get out, I go to live with my parents. My Mom's memory is failing, and my Father fears he won't be able to care for her alone. So I go, to be there for my Dad in his time of need just as he was there for me so many times in my life.

MICHELE

Letter to My Biological Mom

Although I never knew you, your blood runs in my veins. Not just your blood, but perhaps your intellect or humor . . . How much like you am I? Do I look like you? How about quirks? Do I share any of those with you? I must because as I examine those I grew up with, I realize I am nothing like them. I feel like Dr. Seuss's bird that goes around asking, "Are you my mother? Are you my family?"

They say blood is thicker than water, but is it really? Relatively speaking my blood line seems to run pretty thin. First, to be able to cast aside one of your own, then to be unwelcoming for your own to come home?! Really?!!! So all in all, despite my having your blood coursing through me, I feel like making it my own, just mine to share with my children and grandchildren, leaving yours to die out, at least through me. Oh my, I've just set myself free!

NORAJEAN

Maternal Light

I don't know what I would do without my mom. She is my light at the end of every tunnel and the headlights to guide me through. I love how she never passes judgment on me and always forgives me. I wrote her two weeks ago and thanked her for always seeing my beautiful colors when our justice system and DOC only see me in black and white. I am forever grateful to God for putting me in her arms when I was ten weeks old—always and forever.

SUZANNE

The Mother I Never Had

My mother, she is the one who gave me life. There are so many days I beg God and wish she hadn't; she was never really quite a mother. We are alike as much as a screw and screwdriver. We work well together and I love her so much. We are also as different as day and night and both full of anger, hurt and resentment.

I myself have learned to forgive but not forget. My mother on the other hand holds grudges and has never learned to forgive. She's never liked my choices. My drug use is embarrassing and unacceptable. She doesn't understand drugs took her place. I've had so many tears and sleepless nights trying to figure out how to change the past, to fix our future. So you don't hate me so much, my dear mother. Please tell me how to get you to love me or just be okay with me again, to accept me once again, to face me once again. The drugs were the mother I never had.

I'm trying so hard to grow stronger, but with your back turned on me, with your hate and anger, being scared and alone behind these walls, I'm lost and don't know what to do. Can or will I ever please you? I've made wrong choices and took wrong paths; but now I'm back on the right path and need some guidance. And I'm asking for help as a child to a parent. A daughter you gave birth to, as a mother, can you please be my mother, for I am scared to be alone?

I love you even though you can't say the same. A mother's love is supposed to be unconditional. So I thought.

JC

Scars of Your Forgotten Life

You would be with us if it were not for the doctor's messing up and leaving you in my birth canal as long as they did. I was screaming for an emergency C-section, but they would not do it after three hours of pushing to get you out. When you were born, I told them to put you in your father's arms 'cause he was able to come and see you be born. It was hard for him to be there 'cause they had to bring him in chains and cuffs. After about two minutes, he told them to take his little girl 'cause he did not want to hurt you, but he did not know that you were already hurt on the inside and that it was not going to be long before you died. Before he left he named you Faith Hope. Then they took him away, and I was there with you as you took your last breath in my arms. You are our angel watching over us.

BELINDA

Lost in the Dark

A mother lost in the dark trying so hard to grow,
and yet holding on to her child; a child trying so hard
to reach for the light of hope and faith, to understand.

The child sprouts wings to fly upon the light;
the mother looks away into the growing darkness.
The child is torn between love for her mother
and the light that offers help, a future.

Shall she remain in the dark with a mother who lives
with such cold dark emptiness; or go into the light,
become motherless and alone,
but in such a better place?

JOSEPHINE

The Dream and the Hope

I am the dream and the hope
of two twenty-something kids
looking to make their way in this world;
of Daddy's little girl
with tap-dance wishes nestled in cabbage-patch dreams
believing that if I caught the shooting star mid-flight
I would have the wish I wished that night.

Yes, I am the dream and the hope
of eyelashes fallen and whisked away
with a soft blow; dandelion petals sent on a journey
from their stem . . .
With each day I carry possibility
in the tip of my pen;
and with each fall, I carry the wonder
of what may come when I stand right back up again.

I am the dream and the hope
of thirty some-odd years
of understanding the wonderful absurdity
of laughing through tears
of dancing to music to free my soul.
Of giving up, not giving in and daring
to be bold. One day
I will not be here, for this, too, it shall pass;
and I think of then, when I will have made it
through this looking glass.

JILL

Diablo

My dog was ferocious, smart, loving, protective, gentle, sweet. He was my best friend. He went everywhere with me except school or doctor's appointments. He kept the bullies away and brought the friends together. I was little and he did not mind when I climbed on his back and pretended he was my horse. He would patiently go in the direction I prompted him, steering with my hands, clutching tight to his fur. My brothers and sisters tried to make him be horse for them, but he just ended up sitting down when they climbed on. At night he would curl up beside my bed (because my mom would not allow him on the bed) and start his gentle snoring that would lull me to sleep. Sometimes at the end of a particularly long day I would climb down and snuggle in his warm, safe, brown fur; and he would wrap his tail around me in a way that said, "Don't worry. I am here. I will protect you and keep you safe." I loved my dog, Diablo. All these years later when I need a little comfort, I grab my faux-fur blanket and climb down on the floor, wrap up, and fall asleep.

BILLIE

Overnight Grown-up

I cut my sister's Barbie doll's hair and put her toy china in the easy-bake oven. The homemade play-doh Mom made tasted better than the stuff we bought at Ames. Those big fat crayons they gave us at first didn't break as easy as the thin ones when you smashed them with three fingers. My mother had a box of dress-up clothes and would ask me who I was, and had I seen her daughter? I'd cry every time and scream, *It's ME, Mommy! Don't you know it's me?*

When I grew up the next day I was mad. I became the mom; I became the wife; I became the hired hand. I no longer wanted anyone to know. I always had to put on a show. I ran away but wouldn't go far; except the time me and a friend stole her parent's car. I liked to read and did so with greed; and found it would give me a way to get everything I'd need.

I'm forty-two but don't know the same life as you; but when you talk, I can share a story most believe isn't true. I've been through it all but wish I had not; I wish I'd planned my life with a little more thought.

ANGIE

Artwork by Tess

The One Time I Was Finally First in My Class

My face was as red as my blood-soaked pants.
Standing in line to go somewhere I don't even re-
    member.

I was never the first chosen to play games.
I was never the first to be called to the board, 'cause
    I probably really didn't have the answer.
I wasn't the first choice to go to the birthday parties.
I wasn't first on the list when grades were handed
    out.
I wasn't first to find the hidden prize.
I wasn't the first to get in trouble.
But I wasn't the first not to.
I wasn't the first to arrive or the first to leave any-
    where.

But standing there, in line, I was the first to be
    embarrassed,
the first to be heckled,
the first to have the first hint of puberty.

LUCINDA

Life of Lies

I remember in younger days
how my brother had his own caring ways.
Times that we were thrown together,
and others when we were pulled apart.
The cruelties that happened weren't of us two,
but through it all, the two of us, was all I knew.
Memories of people doing mean things—
like the Fletcher brothers making him kiss me.
There were others too, too cruel to share,
but whenever I needed him, he would always be there.
He is there to this day whenever I called.
He picked me up this time when I fell,
and stood right by me as I entered this hell.
The hurt and sorrow I saw cloud his eyes,
as he knew for the first time, my life of lies.
So I guess I've done the cruelest thing of all,
I let the lies of my life make my brother fall.

NORAJEAN

Jingley Bracelets

I was named after you. You were my father's favorite aunt. I've been told I have your spirit and strength. You were eccentric and maybe a bit strange in your ways, a very unique person. I thank you for paving the way! The way you dressed in your jingley bracelets and your vibrant makeup . . . You traveled the world and brought back memories to share with anyone who cared to listen. You, with your long, dark hair and baggy, excessive layered clothes and odd, beautiful scarves, a trait I chose to take up without ever having known you. Your quips and knowledge, I still hear about. The way you were shunned and misunderstood by some, but loved and accepted by most. Thank you for being you and for making it OK to be me.

LUCINDA

Halloween Make-Believe

She thinks back, tries to remember what it was like. There's always the before and after. She was too young to know then. Before he left, Halloween was her favorite holiday. He made it special. They would spend a week decorating the front yard and porch. She shoves leaves in the pumpkin trash bags. He hangs ghost-shaped lights in the bushes. Fills the porch with fake cobwebs and spiders. He never tires, getting every detail right. He makes it special for them. He works all night to create their costumes. Every jewel and sparkle in her sister's crown is perfect.

He paints her face green. Black hat, black gown. Her sister wears all pink: together, good and bad. She laughs. Who would've known back then there would be no good. Just bad. Everything else make-believe, like Halloween memories.

After he left, Halloween stopped. No more decorations. No more trick or treating. No more fun. Just dark. Just her mother's fear and pain. Lights off. No one's home. Take it upon themselves to create their own Halloween. No candy. Just candlelight and the Ouija board. Fake voodoo dolls and haunted basements.

They play in real witch's back yards, hoping to keep the memories alive. They run through her backyard stealing stones, pretending they're cursed. They forget how he made it special. Her memories fade. She grows up. Another day. No parties, no fun. Still living in her mother's fear. Nothing would ever be the same. Her mother's pain cast a shadow over her whole life, forced to keep her mother's skeletons in the closet.

STACY

Silence

I was silent . . . I had no control. A time I could not speak for myself, the fear of being hurt, afraid for me . . . myself! What am I supposed to do? What if he finds me? Is it going to happen again? Please, I pray, watch over me. I need help! I don't know what to do, should I fight back, I don't want to get hurt . . . I have no say, he is the boss, I must obey . . . and remain silent.

MELISSA L

Beautiful Lies

My mother used to force me to look in the mirror and see my beauty. She would tell me to talk to myself, to convince myself that I felt good about my appearance. So I would look in the mirror and lie. I would say *I'm beautiful, I love myself.* Inside, I never believed it. That's what made it easy for people to manipulate me.

But I'm tired. I'm tired of everything—the lies especially. How do you believe in a love based on lies, even if it's only with yourself? I love who I am. But I don't love *how* I am. I force myself to pretend that I enjoy being overweight. I pretend that my personality can outshine my deepest ugliest flaw. But what nobody knows is at night, when I look in the mirror and I see myself, I cry because I want my appearance to match my personality. Why can't I be as beautiful as I feel? I stare at myself. I ask God, *Why, of all flaws, why this?* My weight is nothing compared to this flaw. I feel like if a man was to see it, he wouldn't want me. So I beg God to make it go away, so my face will be beautiful, like a woman's. But it never goes away.

My friends say it's not noticeable. But when I see me, it's the only thing I see. I've gotten through many things. Forced myself to love the ugliest truths about myself. But sometimes it's not enough for me to love myself. Sometimes I just want someone else to love me.

STACY

Gone Forever

We argued incessantly, angry words spoken, hateful and hurtful, until there were no more to be said. Then the silence came, an eerie calm, quietness that hung over us like an ominous black ugly cloud, each of us waiting for the thunder and lightning to clear.

Off to work he went without a sound leaving me to my tears and shame.

I felt, a short time after, a foreboding feeling down deep inside—in my very being. Something was horribly wrong. I made the call—the "I'm so sorry, please forgive me, I didn't mean to cause you pain" call. A few minutes later he was gone forever. Leaving me alone with my guilt and myself.

NORAJEAN

Desirable but Mean

As a young girl, I always wanted a boyfriend, silly as that sounds. I wanted to wear his ring around my neck, have his varsity jacket on my back. I wanted to feel safe and protected. I didn't feel strong on my own, like I am now. When I got my first real boyfriend, I remember being so thrilled that the most popular boy in school wanted to be with me. It was as if the whole world opened up for me. The sun shone brighter, the clouds carried no rain. He was perfect; gorgeous and tall, almost mustached, tan and had a license. He even had rich parents who bought him a Harley for his seventeenth birthday. Even though he wasn't supposed to have me riding on the back, he did.

But, those feelings of awe only lasted for a short three weeks. I quickly became bored with his supposed charm. He had a mean streak and only those who were chosen ever got to see it. He used to hit me, call me names and tell me I was lucky to be with him. At that time, I was extremely let down by the male population, and vowed that even though I may marry (as it turns out, several times) I'd never give my heart away again.

Elaina

He Called Me "Fatty"

When I was in my twenties, my husband would call me a fatty, so I started to make myself puke. Now I see myself differently. I do not care what people think of me or have to say about me. I know that I'm beautiful on the inside and on the outside 'cause my friends tell me so every day that I am.

BELINDA

Shame on You!

Though the words you say aren't true,
they'll always believe you.
When I tell on you, they turn their heads.
What love they give you! Many tears I shed.
I've lived forty years. All say I'm strong.
I exist, is all. My life's all wrong.
I run from you; you drag me back.
You get awards. Shame on you; another attack.
Someday the time will come—I don't know when—
you'll be the one sitting in the pen.
You won't always have the upper hand.
You'll get old; what will you do then?
Reality will hit; you'll be like me.
They won't listen to you, and then you'll see.
You won't have a name or authority.
When they do it to you, how happy I'll be.

ANGIE

Needing Closure

Wanting closure from this long journey, needing closure from his caustic abuse, one fiery word at a time. Packed up place—threw in storage—broke a few laws while absconding my parole. When they got me this time, I am never going home. Not until I can smell freedom in my nose and hear it ringing in my ears. Letting go of the pain which I held to deeply in my chest, as if it were wrapped carefully in its own tourniquet. Often seeping over needing its dressing changed. That pain no longer needed ownership. It was time I let go of that, too. Taking care of me. Enjoying the parts of life that are simple and the parts that aren't—let them go.

TONYA

Remaining Silent

Silence is not guilty vs. guilty.
Silence means no one knows the truth.
I never chose this life of silence. I was forced into it.
The system that should have been my voice
forced me speechless. They were silent
when they placed my life in danger.
Out of anger I've remained silent.
I never say what really happened. At one point
I would've argued the power of silence. Now
I only wish to speak out, to cry out,
to tell everything.

STACY

Sleepover

A boy and girl on top bunk
two girls on the bottom
they share stories
and giggle . . .
just excited to be able to have people over.
Two women in the kitchen;
one has a boyfriend.
The giggles are interrupted by shouts . . .
"Under the bed in the back room"
He's coming . . .
He's almost in here.
The door opens and shuts. . .
There are voices . . .
Arguing . . . mad . . . going to approach
the boyfriend.
There are loud noises.
Like fireworks.
Four children go to see what happened.
A man was being shot.
First bullet tore into his chest.
He kept coming.
When the second and the third hit,
he dropped to the floor
crumpled, broken, still alive.
The children watch,
can't stop it from happening.
A friend of his rushes in . . .
lifts the man's broken body,
twisted in an odd position
into his car.
They go to the hospital.
He doesn't die.
Is still alive.

My brother and I were two of the children.
The man shot was our father.
He wanted to take us with him.
The woman that pulled the trigger
was my aunt.
A part of me died when I saw
bullets ripping into my father's torso.
I am on the path to mend.
I don't understand . . .
Probably never will.
I cannot undo what is done.
I can change my perspective
on things.
I can spend time with my dad
when I get out.
You see, he was also shot in the
head twenty years ago and is blind.
I forgive.
I forgive.
I do.
I do not forget.

LAURA

Life Is a Gift

Life is a gift.
We grow and are given the wings to learn.
Sometimes we fly
yet some other times, we crash and burn.
When we are taught to love, it is hard to hate;
when we are taught to hate, we can't perceive
    anything straight.

LN

Breaking Silence

Silence was what echoed in my life, as a young girl.
I lived in the silence of things not spoken
for so long I became the silence, longing
for a voice, finding
none, frozen with fear.

Oh, but for a comforting word,
a sound, any kind
of vibration from within—a scream
breaks through shattering the silence
of my existence, shards of emotion fall
all around, splinters and slivers,
no whole piece left. I am left
naked for the world to see—
such damaged goods, raw
emotions are my blanket. At last
    the silence
        is broken.

NORAJEAN

Screaming in Silence

Steering wheel in my hand, fist hits my face, mouth clamps shut, tears hit my lap. I still control the car, manage the corner, my cheek is hot. Mind racing. Screaming in my head. Yet silence fills the air. Heavy. Sick of feeling so wrong while longing to feel so right. Lost. Alone. I don't belong anywhere.

HEATHER

Shattered Peace

I. THE SLEEPOUT
Quickly beside me, you fall to peaceful sleep.
And I, brightened, gaze at you care-freely.
Though it is dark, clearly I see your face with my
hand's fair touch, such feeling is captured within me—
and dare be seen by you, all but not too much.
Like an eagle soaring its course, the sound of your
breathing breaks the air's stillness.
And comforted I am through
the quiet hours of the night. Though it is cold,
all the while the warmth of your body stares
at me—offering shelter from the cold
and dampness. No pain from loneliness exists.
Alone indeed I am in thought, but every
thought is shadowed by your presence.
Yes, the beauty of your being keeps me awake—
and too—because I am bewildered . . .
for what reason be this beauty of yours
shared with me?

II. WITNESS TO MURDER

In October 2005 I witnessed a murder in the woods at a makeshift
campsite where I had lived with the would-be murderer. He was so
jealous of my ex-boyfriend that he went to town, tricked him into
coming back to the campsite with him to kill him and to kill him
in front of me. Then he ran away and left me alive.

By the next morning, I checked myself into residential treatment.
My feelings, thoughts, emotions and nerves were all over the place.
There were magnetic words on the refrigerator in the kitchen. I
needed to release, I needed a release. I studied the words for a
couple of days and decided to try to create what I had experienced
using as many of those words as possible. I even copied all of the
words onto a piece of paper so that if I was in my room, I could
still work on creating my experience using only those words. I
found this not only to be quite a task and a test of my patience,
but also, somehow, a small but significant start towards healing
and acceptance.

This senseless murder that I witnessed will always be with me, and is by far the most traumatic event in my life—and I've experienced a few. I don't know that I'll ever heal completely or accept completely . . . but creating this, with the hand I was dealt, so to speak, was somehow very soothing for me and gave me hope for myself.

III. *ABOUT A BANQUET*
The man consumed like wild wind not love,
his secrets were immense.
Dark minute, no sound, say or song for you;
when he did leave and run away.
Yet after the red from you said "Good-bye,"
by evening it was announced how, what, why.
Willing am I if I'm still here,
for this work has promise, through want
up and up.
Signed,
Slender, lace, glass tendril.

AMY

Freedom

At peace with the world,
loving yourself and others,
to me, is freedom.

MICHAELA

Disguised Blessing

Drunk and high
I'm a good-time girl,
it's time to fly,
want to give it a whirl?

That was me,
Sometime back.
It was sad to see,
I got off track.

My life was simply not my own.
I was someone I didn't know.
For sins, I must atone,
this is really going to blow.

It must be done,
and quickly, too.
From this I cannot run.
It's just what I must do.

I let people down,
made a mess of my life.
I embarrassed my hometown,
and I wasn't a good wife.

I've spent my life in a bar
always getting loaded
I crashed my car,
my whole life exploded.

Just one more drink,
just one more oxy.
No time to think,
I was stuck, as if with epoxy.

I couldn't manage
all alone.
Then I met a badge
even then, I was stoned.

It's over now
I've learned my lesson.
I can see how
it's all a disguised blessing.

ELAINA

Homeless Person's Interview

"Where do you live?"
"Gosh. I don't want to say."
When you say *I'm homeless*, they always look with
    dismay.
"Where was your last place of residence?"
Now it's getting intense.
"What's the address of yesterday's stay?"
"How long did you stay there?"
I look down. "Just a day."
"Do you have any close family?"
I look up. "Hell, yes! I've got many."
"What's your means of income?"
The look she gives says she thinks I am dumb.
"I fly a sign I put out on a can."
"Isn't that a crime?" "Not where I sit. It's just fine."
"What's some of your goals?"
"I'd like some shoes without holes."
"What's your future plan?"
"It's to be just as I am."

ANGIE

Shattered Trust

Abused from age four to eleven by uncles, a friend of the family, my
mother's cousin, and my brother's father. The last time a neighbor-
hood boy attempted to rape me while two of his friends held me
down, my sister and boyfriend in the room. Why didn't they help?
Why didn't they or I scream? We were in shock. A shattered trust
that can never be regained. My mom believed me and others didn't.
It hurts. You feel ashamed although you have no reason to be.

JEN

Rebel Crush

I had the biggest crush on one of my sister's friends. At the time, I was sixteen years old, in high school. I would always rush home, hoping he would be there hanging out with my sister. And he frequently was.

I learned all his favorite music, all of his pastimes, and all of his character traits. After about five months of this obsessive behavior, I finally grew the nerve to express my feelings. In private, of course. Much to my surprise, I became his girlfriend. At that moment in time is when my life took a turn for the worse.

He was a rebel, very stubborn, always thought he was right, fought with his parents, hardly went home, and he lived in the back woods. The type to ride four-wheelers, hunt, target practice, fishing in the dark. Before too long, I was cutting time short with all of my friends, extra-curricular activities and homework to spend more time with him. And he encouraged it. We could find better things to do than sit in class. And we did.

My grades crashed. I had no regard for what was right anymore. Nothing mattered. My family strongly discouraged me from engaging in a relationship with him due to all the trouble he caused. But the harder I tried to stay away from him, the closer I was drawn to him. Our relationship had its ups and downs for a total of three-and-a-half years, until we finally ruined each other. Although it turned out the way it did, the place that time holds in my heart left a scar deep enough to last a lifetime.

Melissa G

Addiction

Instant gratification. I fill the empty void
with something worse than nothing.
I lost myself for a long time, and finally
was able to see life differently.

Why oh WHY is life so hard? To watch somebody
dying from a disease and having the antidote
in your hands, saying, PLEASE take this
and they won't. That's addiction. The Devil.

The easiest thing I've ever done.
Sucks the life out of you and those who love you.
Is where I go when afraid and helpless.
Hunger and happiness. Pain just disappears.
Oh, that feeling I get in my belly.
Oh, how that feels! Pain is why I love you
so much, I never seem to get enough.
Addiction.

A GROUP EFFORT,

EACH WOMAN CONTRIBUTING

A LINE WITHOUT SEEING THE PREVIOUS ONE

Belle of the Ball

My own best critic as I down another beer,
laughing without fear.
Everybody loves me, I am fun,
beautiful woman dancing in the sun.
Snorting that ball of cocaine—more beer feels great—
all eyes on me as I take center stage.
I am the belle of the ball, make the crowd laugh;
as the sun rises I soon see just half
myself in the mirror against the entrance wall.
My reaction of disdain and disbelief makes me stall:
who the hell is that staring back at me?
Up all night—the belle of the ball—she
now appears to have been hit
with a string of bowling balls lit
with the stale smell of cigarettes lined
through each lock of curly hair—mine!
My clothes stink of stale beer.
Another day missed at work, it's clear.
Could there be a solution for this
just-give-me-one-more-milligram miss?
I am not sure what to say to my man,
all because I had to party again.

TONYA

Faces Looking Back at Me

When I was getting so high off my drugs and alcohol, all I could do was see so many faces looking back at me. It was scary for the first couple of times that it happened, until my body got used to the idea of what was going on with it. Then I just started to get more high so I could see the faces looking back at me.

It was as if I thought they were friends or my family looking at me and trying to tell me to stop. But I never listened to them. I still see my faces looking at me even when I'm not high or drunk. But the faces I see now are angels and God watching over me.

BELINDA

Consumed

We have worked so hard for it, though.
It seems like what we wanted was far away.
Always grasping, reaching for it.
It made me so stressed out at times.
It distracted me from life as I kept desiring that
   which I wanted.
At first, I was excited about it.
Then it seemed to turn into a job itself in order to
   attain it.
Yet, I still wanted it no matter what.
Every day that went by, it made me want it more
   and more.
What was going on around here?
I became a former image of myself.
Consumed by what I wanted.
I forgot everything that I needed.
What I wanted was the most important thing to me.
I had to obtain it or I would go insane!
I said to myself, *just let me have one more day.*
That's all I need was one last time to hold it in my
   hands.
One last time to make me feel numb and happy
   all at once.
One last time to cherish it and for it to satisfy me.
After that last time, I still wanted to have it.

But, what we want is never that simple.
What we need always seems to be waiting, right
   around the corner.

RAVEN

Crawling on My Knees

You've taken every ounce of dignity. When you gave me your super powers, you gave me the power, the good morning America power lines that reached out to broken homes across my area. Standing by, watching at your own mercy squeezing out the vital thoughts that it was wrong, and you made me believe it was right. You showed me your support by making it easier to take care of my family, with the money the power gave; tiny seals, all the promises you made. But in the end when I was low down and tired you picked me up, and see I guess it's not that bad, it's like ten cups of coffee you gave me. I can function. Look at the money I have, the friends gave me security too, but then the super powers turned away from them, I couldn't suck out the power from their lives, so there went the friends, my children too. You watched it cause me pain and you didn't care, you continued to feed me, to the point I couldn't function, I couldn't live my life because the power took over and made a monster out of me. I turned my back on my family, they were the last to go, you had me at your mercy, crawling on my knees, you brought me over the threshold of hell and left me there to die. Giving up those super powers you gave me has brought me back. Stronger than even not needing those super powers to get through life. Watching your reflection fade away has given me a brand new perception on life. Free and clean to live happily without the super powers that took my life away from me.

TESS

"Savored and shared . . ."[1]

Reminds me of my drug abuse when I have it. I savor it, share it with my BF and then always have to have more. It is always an on-going, all-day, 24/7 cycle that never stops on its own will.

I don't know why this happens to me. I am the outcast in my family. Why can't it be Erica, Amanda, or Shawn? Why does it have to be ME? What did I do wrong to deserve this addiction?

God has it in for me, he will test my success and determine my reincarnation. I try to succeed, but always fail. Freedom for me only means failure in progress.

KH (DECEASED 2012)

---

[1] "Savored and shared, and asked for more," a line from Grace Schulman, "Apples," *The Unbroken String* (New York: Houghton Mifflin, 2007).

Caged

I don't know myself anymore.
Can you help me open these doors?
Why do I cry myself to sleep at night?
Why have I let drugs take over my light?
I'm so scared and all alone;
it's by myself that I roam,
not able to slow the breathing as I run
from beatings, rapings and this angry man carry-
    ing a gun.
I've lost a childhood spent in rage
and now I sit here inside a cage.
I seek the life I once knew
on the streets with my crew:
robbing, fraud and all that fun,
a life I brought myself up in on the run.
I can't remember every day;
I cannot tell you everything per se
but as of now, I sit and rot.
It's time for God that I sought;
for what though another lie be told
when I get out, the same show; and behold
a lifer my father raised me
not even to be free.
So I sit here and really don't care;
I'd do it all over even if I'd been sober.

Flip

I Take Myself Back

I take myself back from you—
you, evil—I despise you,
never want to see you again.
You took everything I had,
everything good in my life
has disappeared.

I take myself back
to the days I was free from you,
I was happy, smart, confident;
honest, loyal and trustworthy.

I take myself back to my family.
You'll never hurt me again.
I might want you but I remember—
remember when you made me so ill—
when you made me lie and steal and
hurt the people I loved.

LAURA

∽

I Never Dreamed of Defeat

I used to have a loving, handsome husband. I never pictured myself
as his wife or anybody else's wife. The idea of marriage as an institution was nothing I could ever believe in, as if always knowing
I could not be a better half. He had compassion and faith in us,
while I always looked for reasons to doubt. My half-heartedness
cheated us both. I learned I could not conquer love. But without
it, I am defeated.

BS

∽

Just One Chance

For years I longed for . . . someone to call me mom, look up to me for advice, guidance, send them to school. I finally got that opportunity and I fucked up worse than I ever could have. I'm sitting in jail with no one to call my own. I mean, I know they're MY children. But do *they* know that? I mean, they were so young. I know seventeen more years of this hell will be pure torture, not having them in my life. But I still long for the day when I can finally see them, hug them, and let them know what they really mean to me.

It's amazing how you can long for something so bad, and in a split second have it be torn away like it was never a part of your life.

One chance is what I need; just one opportunity to prove myself, prove that I am worthy. I am a good person, mother. Why won't anybody give me that?

I know that I will see them again, so I guess maybe that's what I long for now. Just to see them again. I know when it finally happens, nobody will ever take that feeling away from me. EVER.

L—O—N—G—I—N—G . . .

DEBI

Artwork by Tiffany H

I Got What I Wanted

I wanted to figure out a way to live my day to day life and not dread getting out of bed every single morning. I wanted to do what I wanted to when I wanted to do it. I wanted to not worry about paying rent, feeding myself, or putting gas in the car.

I wanted to get high, stay high, and never ever have to go without being high.

I wanted to have a book published. I wanted to make my father proud. I wanted to do something bigger with my life than the mundane, barely-get-by paycheck, pay bills, eat, sleep and do-it-again existence I feared so much. But mainly, I just wanted a break from the intense pressure of all these wants . . .

Now I am enclosed within walls 24 hours/day; no bills to pay, no worries about my next meal, or putting gas in my car. No worries about barely getting by on my paycheck; there is no getting by on $2/day. So yeah, in some ways, I guess I got what I wanted.

JILL

Learning to Love Myself

When I was young, I fell in love. But that time it wasn't myself. It was a horrible drug. Its name was Oxy80. I had started going downhill 'til I hit rock bottom. Oh, man, did that hurt! I lost everything, including myself. But with help, support and time, I found myself again. Now I am still young and I have fallen in love again. And guess what? It was myself who I had fallen in love with. I am now a mother of two boys. I'm caring, respectful, loving, faithful, fun, outgoing, understanding and I never get enough sleep. But I would never trade it for anything, because I now love myself!

TG

Crystal Church

The clear plastic church lit up and sparkled like crystal when I turned on the switch. It also played the music from *Silent Night*. It was the most beloved Christmas gift I had ever received. Not only because it was given to me by Santa himself, but because Santa seemed to be pointing me directly toward the one and only hope that could change my life.

I have always loved God. I have always loved Jesus. Now, for the first time, not only did I have hope in God, but I realized God had hope for me. Every night I would switch the little church on, listen to the gentle hymn and watch the lights twinkle as I prayed.

BILLIE

Losing My Brother

Above the stars, although the constantly falling trails all so pretty may not be not the paths led to much blood shed before I've got to pull over for sure my eyes are full of tears I can't see in my mirrors I've got to let it all out with out a doubt I know I got to go on where is my magic wand to put it all back together like I need it to be like before like someone had to open up this door of horror movie only for real and I feel it threw my heart and don't know where to start to get it to stop and I use to run hard in the fast lane and I'm sitting here stuck and can't even get to my truck so what the fuck do I do really how do I ever get back to feeling silly and funny and happy is even right when I'm so mad and hurt my world is wrecked last I checked I still believed in God he however really let me down with this I can't for the life of me figure out why he took my brother or even better yet my brother's son's father from him. God, I trust and believe in you, God, still after this. Jesus—Amen.

TH

Beach Bust

As I look at my father's blue eyes, he tells me, "Get ready, I have a surprise!"

My lil' sister, just an infant, father remarried, we pack the car up with supplies for our trip.

A trip to Hampton Beach. I get so excited, never having been to a beach before. I hear the whoosh of the waves, seagulls chirping and flying, the smells of the salt water.

As we're all loaded into the car, I sit next to my baby sister, entertaining her two-second attention span.

We finally arrive at Hampton Beach and it's crowded with families and friends, all enjoying the hot summer sun.

After driving around for what seemed like an eternity, we found a motel. It wasn't the best, but Dad said, "Girls, we'll make the best out of it." We all agreed.

Then it was mayhem. One thing went wrong after another. First my dad locked the keys in the trunk, trying to get them out every way he could possibly think of. He broke the radio antenna off to slim-jim the window, finally retrieving the keys. Next we go to the beach . . .

My little toes in the hot sand, staring out at what seems an endless sight of water, so blue and clear. My thoughts and fascination are broken by my stepmom yelling for my dad—my li'l sister Tia was sitting in the sand and a wave came up and started to take her away. As always, my dad was right there and caught her. She was frightened as we all were, so Dad said, "Let's pack up and go home!"

Our trip was so short-lived. I was devastated. I didn't even get to feel the water of the ocean, let it burn my eyes or get in my mouth. My trip to the ocean was officially done. I was so upset, I cried. And then to make matters worse, due to Dad breaking the antenna off, we sat in near silence for hours upon hours.

SHAWNA B

Wheel

It feels like my life is a wheel; but it's not going
  anywhere at all.
It feels like I'm staying in one place all the time. I
  don't like it at all.

JESS

My Heart, My Well

My heart is a deep well.
Hope and love splatter my insides.
Hate and regret live there, too.
Dark scars from self spread thin
unable to recognize myself.
Looking deep within
there's barely a trace,
a faint glimpse of me deep in that well.

It's me splattered everywhere,
everything I once believed in worn out.
Self fading. My well filling
with something I don't recognize.
My heart, solid around the edges.
The middle still gold.
Why is my deep well drying up?
I'm suffocating myself. Suppressing
everything I am. All the wonderful things
about who I am slowly sinking
to the bottom of my wishing well.
Lost and forgotten,
shimmering only once in a while,
if the sun hits it just right.
A short glimpse, a flicker of who I was
not too long ago. Then it fades. Back
to dark, to deep.

All my features, blurry lines. I fade
dark blue. Light blue. Some shade of grey
then white. Nothing transparent. I hold
secrets that no one can see. Just feel
in my deep shades of blue. I'm worn down
almost smudged out. Worn thin.
Blank stare. Don't look down.
I fear I might see that shimmer,
small glimpse of self looking out
from deep within.

STACY

A Chance to Shine

When I was young I had dreams of Future Me. I could see a writer, a singer, or maybe a mother. Someone with worth to the world. Someone who would be remembered as a benefit, or a person to look up to. Not revered, just appreciated. As I looked forward, I could see me accomplishing this for my kids and the ones that I love. To look into their eyes and see pride and love. But what I see now is contempt and sadness. I have no control over what has passed; yet I am totally responsible. I may have been lied about. No one cares to hear the truth.

So here I sit, unable to change what has passed. Always looking to the future. Hoping for the dream to unfold. Waiting for my turn to see the pride. Hoping for my chance to shine.

Lucinda

Bottom Feeder

You were always right and never could be wrong.
You always led, never would you follow along.

You hear a song and sing back;
you see white and think black.
You try reading between the lines,
always end up paying fines.

Consequence for a crime you're sure
you didn't commit, you sit with it
too long; and it lasted.
You're a blast to be with
when in a good mind frame.
Got a good heart. Start thinking
on top of the world, get off the bottom
feeder you're no cheater. No need to beat her
up any more. Love her, treat her right. Give her
2 blue *I love you's* tonight.

TH

My Father Told Me So

Things people have told me
have turned out to be true
as I sit here with these women
I have never once knew.
I was told I'd turn out to be a lifer
my father once said a time or two.
Just look at me now, here in this jail
with the same attitude.
I sit here and try to stay out of trouble
but as they said, trouble be my middle name.
As I give in and play their stupid little game,
the hole being my second home,
I wish and I pray this bitch be blown away
by that big nasty cyclone; but truth be told
I'll sit here 'til I get old
with all these so-called friends
that say they have your back; in the end
that turn out to be rats and bitches
who only pretend.
So say it again, father, about my future be told.
I'll die all alone, with my heart icy cold.

FLIP

Lone Wolf

I felt that I was a lone wolf growing up 'cause I never had anyone to be there for me after being raped at the age of 8 by what was supposed to be a family friend. But now I am learning that I am not alone any more. That I do have friends, and can make new ones if I want to let them in. Yes, it is hard to trust anyone, but you have to start down a new road; 'cause if not, you will always be in the shadow of a lone wolf like I was. More and more I have overcome that thanks to friends and family. I don't want to walk down that path ever again.

BELINDA

Cracked Heart

Heart cracked. Split. Old. Dead. Self-inflicted wounds. Every groove represents life's struggles. My burdens buried deep within the channels. Hidden in the cracks. My channels carry secrets and lies no one should know. My cracks hold truths that are decaying my head from inside out. My years are young but my heart is old. If you counted all the rings, that's the lifetimes my heart has seen. Pain in every ridge. It's amazing it's still whole. It loves a little less. I thought age and pain would allow me to love. But truth is my heart no longer pumps love, but pumps hate instead. It's not red and warm. It's not a cozy place to be. It's grey, cold and ugly. Filled with lifetimes of truth. Filled with history, filled with past. It is no longer light with life. But heavy with death.

STACY

Jaws of Regret

Oh, to live my life one step ahead of myself—
to know the actions that will bring joy or pain.
But now regret holds me in its biting jaws.
I feel the teeth sinking in, wishing I could
retrace my steps to start my journey afresh;
but the teeth sink deeper and my foolish wishes
cannot help me escape regret's bitter hold.

DANA

Among Sharks

I lay in bed at night and I stare at myself. My reflection broken up by thick metal bars. I stare awkwardly and persistently trying to force myself to recognize the person staring back at me. I'm not sure who I am anymore. Most times I avoid my reflection. I wanna avoid who I've become. I see betrayal and defeat staring back at me. A lifetime of pain. In my reflection I see infinite street wisdom, loyalty, honor. All my street morals slappin' me in my face. The games ethics laughing at me. If only I had known there wasn't any rules to this game.

My throat cut wide open, I'm bleeding; but no one cares. I'm alone. A goldfish among sharks. A sheep in wolf's clothing. I try to blend but my heart gives me away. She is scared. She's confused, forced to be someone she wasn't. Made to believe it was the only way.

I would give anything to show her different, to keep her safe. I would give anything to go back to her to save her from him, from herself. She looks so scared, but I know she is brave. I know, cuz we survived. Only now my hope is fading and I'm accepting of my life amongst sharks. I know how to take care of us now.

STACY

Broken

. . . beyond shedable tears—or rateable pain—I'd spend hours weeping—alone. My mother was dying, my family in ruins, my breath stolen. So young—so scared, so alone. Jumping from the window, particles of dander explode in the cascades of luminous simplicity. Her tabby coat so soft, her eyes so understanding and calm. As I'd watch her approach, her methodical prowl soothed my inner distress. Her wet nose so forcefully nuzzled against my cheek as to say, "You're not alone." Her circular dance to find her resting place so random, but as she'd flop down beside me, she always found our "niches."

In a time I felt so unsure of everything and everyone, her presence reminded me—composure, resilience, companionship. I was in such denial as to the elephant in the room that, in those moments, those interactions she taught me much more than I'll ever realize. That she was almost saying, "I'm here, I'm not leaving, and although we both know what's in store—we'll have each other."

I lost my faith in humanity and regained it all the same, all because she heard the words I couldn't speak, took the pain I couldn't bear alone, and knew that I needed her.

There still lives a pain that can never be healed, never be accepted or forgotten. Where that lies also houses an anger, a rage, a guilt, an irrational self-entitlement, that burns bright but hidden in shadows. I made bad choices, hurt those I loved because I felt alone and scared. Before I found my voice, I found a monster—engulfing and brash. I keep that being close enough to remind myself who I was, who I am, who I've yet to become.

JS

Captured by Fire

Lost in a dream—twisting, fighting
my way away from something
that burns. I can't force myself
to look at it. Colors surround me,
engulfing me. It's beautiful but
it hurts. I don't understand how
something so beautiful can be
so painful. Suddenly a thought comes
to mind: I'm burning to death;
the fire has captured me
long enough to take my life along
with my dreams, a sad story of fiction
that feels all too real.

CV

Drowning in Life

So many of my years drowning in a sea of life, coming up for air
once in a while when I couldn't weather the storm. The light so
close, yet always so far away. The waves of life pushing at me from
both sides. Struggling to breathe, knowing surely the end is near.
When would I realize it was just a sea of my own tears and fears?
And reaching out for help made the storm clear. Or was it some
divine intervention from above? The answer to that I will never
know, but continue to live my life grateful either way.

JD

Don't Fall in Love with Me

Don't fall in love with me.
I snap a sting like that of a black scorpion.
Don't ask me to hold you.
My bite is deadly like that of a black widow spider.
I'll weave my web around your soul,
like that of a brown recluse,
only to prey on every move you make,
like that of a mountain lion.
Don't try to act like me.
I'm very rare and extinct,
like that of a fire breathing dragon.
Don't call me names,
for I spew venom like that of a Komodo dragon.
Don't try to sneak by me.
I sway side to side until I'm right behind you,
like that of a shark.
Don't think I'm alone.
I travel in packs like that of a litter.
Don't think you can trust me.
I stick by my own with an unbreakable bond
like that of a mother bear.
Don't try to outrun me.
I am swift as a wolf.
Don't think you're better than everyone.
You're just a token on the food chain,
like that of the animal kingdom.
Don't call me ugly,
for I have many beautiful colors
like that of a peacock.
Don't keep the lights on,
because I love the dark,
to see where I'm going like that of a bat.
But, all in all, I'm cute, soft, warm and cuddly
like a newborn puppy.

AT

I Just Knew

Up until now, I've always trusted myself. I always listened to what my body was telling me about the situation. Sometimes I just know things before they happen. Like my house getting raided. Somethin' in me tells me, "hide everything." I'm ready when the door goes down. They leave empty-handed. How do I know? I just know. It scares my friends. They stop trustin' me. They question me. How do you explain intuition?

There was the time in the taxi. I got arrested with all these grams. I had faith in the universe that things would be OK. I didn't over react. Maybe it was shock, but my silent prayers worked. I think it's about intentions *vs.* actions. If your heart is good, then you stand a good chance.

But like I said, up until now, I trusted myself.

I remember the man, the one who set me up.

I remember him, his hands shaking, his crooked smile.

I remember the sweat beads on his forehead.

I remember my body saying, "NO."

I remember ignoring myself. And taking the $500.

I remember the hallway, the hesitation. It was so subtle, but it was there. I had so many things clouding my judgment. The biggest one was paranoia. I thought everyone was Leon. Everyone was coming for my head. So I didn't trust what my body told me. And I played the fool. I ended up in jail. Alone and heart-broken.

But I have faith in time and in the process I went through. Everything happens for a reason.

I trust that everything will be OK.

STACY

Brokenhearted Valentine[2]

I wasn't ready to look love in the eyes.
I turned from its awkward stare, as if being ogled
by a stranger.
It was snowing large fluffy flakes, like cotton clouds
drifting from the sky.
I'd probably walked forever that night, pacing my
kitchen, afraid to sit with my feelings for fear of
what may be revealed.
Five miles on cardboard soles would have seemed
like gliding on air compared to that endless
walking on white linoleum with yellow flowers
etched in the middle.
The boy behind me must have vanished, like one
of those cotton shimmering clouds I saw in my
streetlight, from my second story window.
He tried hard to muffle the sound of his disappoint-
ment as I disappeared into the white abyss.
The sound as he ripped his own big heart in two
fell on deaf ears, a mirage in the clouds.
The part he handed me said only, WHY?

SUZANNE

---

[2] Modeled on Cathy Bowers, "How I Became an Existentialist," *A Book of Minutes* (Oak Ridge, TN: Iris Publishing Group, 2004).

My Fate Is Everywhere

Everywhere I look, I see my fate.
When I look in your eyes
and you uncomfortably turn
away from my gaze.

In the pool of water I've mishappenly left
on the bathroom floor; or the mirror
that is cracked and faded, making it hard
to see your true reflection.

Everywhere I look I see my fate—
when I sense your fear,
when I smell your uncertainty
in the taste of your resentment
that you force me to swallow
as if it were mine—it leaves
a dry lump in my throat.

The snow that covers the ground
as I aimlessly drive down dirt roads
with no direction.

Suzanne

Junky Mom

It's hard to believe I have two beautiful babies. Who would ever know considering that I, their mother, do not care for them the way mothers do. I, a selfish, rotten, junky, drug-addicted mother, care more for drugs than my children. I know what you're thinking, "How can a mother be so heartless?" And I can't answer you! I know it's an awful thing, but at least I can admit it. I wish it were not true. I have lost everything and didn't care, but I tell you now— there is only time left to care about my children and not myself, and that means doing what it takes to keep my family together.

KH (DECEASED 2012)

Burning Anger

As I look out my window I see what I have allowed my life to be. I no longer can see the sway of the trees or the vulnerability of the earth's breeze. Instead I see razor wire and fencing with guards telling us to go lock in.

The anger burns within my soul, swallowing my pride, leaving a hole, wounds so deep no one can see the bottom. Tears add up leading to oceans of sorrow, rivers of drugs, seas of pain, wishing I could go back to that first day. I don't know who I am anymore, what I have allowed myself to become, why I am sitting in this cell all alone.

The orange of the flame burns bright like the intensity of my heart for you. Chains shackle my soul as I drop to my knees wishing you knew how I feel, but my screams go unheard. Why can't you tell I love you.

AT

Trying to Find My Place

Noticeably erratic, silently open, screaming nothingness . . . Apparent pain behind a thousand masks of a smile. I see me in the serenity of the clean spaces. I see me in the chaos of the rapidly blotched darkness—everywhere and nowhere. I'd like to follow the direction to the appropriate destination. However, my lines aren't straight and I can't seem to follow a damn thing lately. How would I know it will lead to the right spot? I ramble in my word and art. Internally distraught and emotionally vulnerable . . . I'm just trying to find my place, where I am, in what I see.

LM

Day to Night

Evening comes in softly
spreading
through the sky,
gray moving in
as the blue begins to die.
Watch it,
watch it closely,
always in your sight;
but who can say
the moment
when day has
turned to
night?

SARAH

Imprints

Leaves make imprints
like my hands leave fingerprints.
My blue veins run visibly through
like old leaves.
I hold the future in the palm of my hand
but I am no fortune teller.
I seek footprints to follow.

BS

Reflection

Relationships are reconsidered from the distance of incarceration, with its many hours to ponder, worry, question, and yearn. Poignant tales of missed family milestones figure here alongside the realities of life on the inside, with its boredom, isolation, fears, and struggles with inner demons. Living and working inside a system rife with pressures, such as bullying and manipulative power, illuminate both the psychic imprisonment within and the physical prison where 170 women live in close quarters. Toward the end of this section, growing self-understanding is pitted against challenges of often dysfunctional relationships and show up in anxious prayers and raw pleas as women anticipate returning to those environments. As a woman prepares for release from prison, she often shares a strong connection to the natural world as it contributes to understanding human relationships. And, as she becomes determined to leave incarceration behind for good, her writing turns to newly discovered faith and spirituality, often in the form of prayers, dreams, or visions for her future.

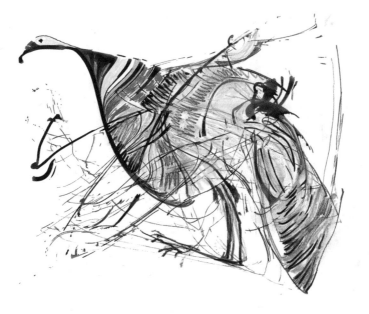

Artwork by Jeanne

The Bird of Hope

I remember the colors, so deep and vibrant. The most beautiful creature I've ever seen; I think a bird. The one, the something I've been asking for. Some people get genies or fairy godmothers. I got the most magnificent, splendid creature.

STACY

Merely Me

They say, "crazy, nuts, cuckoo," yet they whisper,
  "shh, she's mentally ill."
They say, "off my rocker, in la-la land," yet they
  whisper, "shh, she's mentally ill."
They say, "messed up, screwed up," yet they whisper, "shh, she's mentally ill."
I hear labels "depressed and anxiety," yet they whis-
  per, "shh, she's mentally ill."
More labels are heard "traumatized, shock," yet
  they whisper, "shh, she's mentally ill."
I begin to whisper, "smart, confident, a good person
  and mom." Yet I think, " I am mentally ill."
My safe place is not very safe, since I am "mentally
  ill."
Why am I crouching? I must be "crazy, nuts, and
  oh yeah, mentally ill."
I start to breathe, yet I breathe as though I am
  anxious because "I am mentally ill."
Why am I "mentally ill"?
Why are we whispering?
How come they decided "I am mentally ill"?
I stand up and say my name and they look my way.
I say, "I am not perfect, is all."
I raise my voice and say, "I am a person whose feel-
  ings are topsy-turvy, is all."
I shout, "I am me and I love who I am!"
They look at me and say, "see, she's mentally ill,
  take her away!"
I go to my safe place where I crouched and could
  hardly breathe.
I whisper, "I am not mentally ill, I am just merely
  me."

RAVEN

Relearning Trust

My fear of loving another human closes me off. I have become jaded, spiteful, resentful of not having the capacity to truly love another person. I fear being wounded emotionally by another's words or actions. My desire to love has not been extinguished, just my ability to do so. I feel closed off to so much, not only people but resources, as well. I feel that I am a weaker person for all my negativity when, years ago, I was so positive. I was ready and able to work, learn, grow as a person . . . and love unconditionally. I've learned, mostly from this class, that I need to be more open to others' and my own feelings. I need to relearn the art of trust so that I may once again become a whole person.

ELAINA

"Marvelous error"[1]

Long before the alcohol, the nicotine, the needle, I escaped and soothed with macaroni and cheese, hot dogs, and Egg McMuffins. I would fill the pain with pasta, escape with eclairs, de-stress with Doritos.

It was my first addiction; not unlike my first words or my first steps, it was the building block of my shack of isolation. It was my first magnificent plan to hide from the world by getting bigger. I would immediately follow this up with crash diets, thinking that if I could get control of this, I would have control of my entire life.

What a twisted little game of indulgence and instant gratification that would continue into my adult years, only the stakes became much higher than gaining ten pounds. The stakes became life and death, Russian roulette with a syringe.

Win or lose, there was no end until one day, as in Monopoly, my Chance Card came up—go to jail, directly to jail. I did not pass "Go" and certainly did not collect $200 . . . instead I got to stop playing the game. And what a "marvelous error" it has been, to retire my jersey, to step to the sidelines, to sit back and stop playing. Yes, what a marvelous error, what a delicious mistake.

Jill

---

[1]Antonio Machado (1875–1939), "Last Night As I Was Sleeping," in *Risking Everything: 110 Poems of Love and Revelation*, ed. Roger Housden (New York: Harmony Books, 2003), 118.

Demons

As I sit on my unit, all I hear is yelling, all I see is cutting, and it makes me want to do it all over again. It is hard for me to get past all these demons, but I need to stay hopeful as I see them cut their selves—that I can manage to control my feelings, so I can fight off all of these demons that are fighting to get out of me so I will hurt myself . . . but I can't accept any of these feelings because I feel it is just not me talking or feeling. This is like a different person in me, so I'm going to fight as hard as I can to stop clinging to this control that is over my head.

I wish I could accept what the demon made me do when I was thirteen years old. I got drugged up and had sex for the first time and got pregnant. I wish I never got pregnant, but that baby made me do more drugs 'cause I had her and gave her away. It was so hard for me. The demons got me so high, but also made me lose a very precious part of me, and I know I cannot change that. I lost myself and a child at a young age 'cause of drugs.

BELINDA

∾

My Name Is Not Conformity

I had always been ashamed
when I was a young child
so wild and untamed
like a horse in the wild.
I learned who I *should* be,
and how I *oughta* act
if I was going to fit in
and stop feeling so out of whack.
I just couldn't play the part, though,
no matter how good an actress.
To me their world wasn't a nice "act," so
I remained an outcast mess.

As I grew older,
I became who *I* became.
Not some mindless drone-like soldier.
I was someone with a name!
I dressed so rather oddly,
weird some—most—would say.
To know why they always stared at me,
that's why I'd dress and act that way.
They always tried to make me conform.
Sorry, but my name is not conformity.
Their world is just so foreign.
I'll just stay in my "weird" upside-down, topsy-
    turvy world
all because that's me.

VALERIE

History's Hell

All the time it's how I was, not how I am.
I change my life. I change my ways.
Then I look to them in hopes for praise,
but instead they reminisce of my troubled days.

All alone, though I'm in a crowd,
the thought of what they think brings on my shroud.
Some ask what I do; with excitement I tell.
Then someone says, "she's known for blah-blah-blah"
and back I go to history's hell.

All through the times I try to prove them wrong.
Once again I'm in jail, I'm told it's where I belong.
Some people here have known me for years; I'll try
    my best
to set them right. I'll try so hard both day and night.
But some still say I give a fright.

All was well and I was going strong.
And then I blew it. I did something very wrong.
Now the ones who talk to me are the ones who
shouldn't want to and the ones who
for me hung the moon, put me in a cocoon.

All back I am in history's hell.
Will I ever again get out, I cannot tell.
The guilt, mistrust and anger and pain swell.
And if I give change, they lock me in one of their cells.

All I want is good for people to see.
Why do they bring up shit and embarrass me?
Should they have to know the hell in me?
Why can't they keep quiet and let good be.

ANGIE

Maybe Prayers Don't Really Get Answered

Sometimes I wonder if God hears me. Maybe He's tired of me . . . Maybe I'm tired of Him, tired of silence, of never knowing what to do. How do I trust in Him, when I barely trust in myself . . . I just cry to Him, but He never responds. So maybe I did something wrong. If He's waiting for me to figure it out on my own, I can't . . . Well, I haven't yet at least . . . I'm not caught between desire and fear any more. Just locked in regret. Stuck in hate. I feel the further I try to run from it, the closer it comes to consuming me entirely. I'm tryna keep my head above water. I been drowning slowly for twenty-two years. I'm tired of fighting. I'm not sure I have any strength left. I still have some tiny piece of hope in me, cuz somewhere inside me, I know God hears me.

I don't know what's taken Him so long . . . why can't He save me from myself. Maybe prayers really don't get answered. Why keep hoping for something that we know will never happen? I'm just tired and confused. How can so much pain and suffering be part of some beautiful plan, a plan we never know about until after it's unfolded? Why can't He give me directions? It would make things easier for me. Why bring me this far to leave me?

My hope and my belief that everything happens for a reason got me through all the years of madness. Now I'm not sure there is a reason for anything. It's what we tell ourselves to get by. My whole life is just a series of random unfortunate events that created this mess of who I am . . . What if my life and my pain is just entertainment for God?

STACY

Back to the Rabbit Hole

For so long, he deceived, she couldn't see the light;
for so long she believed that everything would be
    all right.
Every day she cries; every night she mourns.
Her fears proved to be right—
her whole world has been torn.

She lowers her head, now blind to her future; she
    only knows her side of the pain.
The tears she cries feel like such torture.
She watches her burning photos in their glitter
    frames.
Where is there to go when the rabbit hole ends?
You go back to what you know
not caring how THAT ends.

Her rope is tight, it's grown thin, emotions spilling
    over like a flood.
She loved him 'cuz she loved him, just because she
    could.
World of darkness, no more sun; she scars herself,
    you see;
she speaks in the third person so she can forget
    that she's me.

But this is now, and that was then;
I've finally set her free.
Her heart, her soul has been mended.
She's finally glad to be me.

VALERIE

My Handwriting Is Mine

My writing is curvy and slanted, almost unreadable to everyone else's eyes. But to my eyes, I can read it just fine. My kids say it's worse. My boyfriend just guesses, and my mom, not so proud of my penmanship. But I've had it my whole life. It's the one thing that I know won't change in my life, and I wouldn't want it to. It's what defines me. It's mine.

> *Haiku:*
> Had it my whole life
> The one thing I know won't change
> It's what defines me

MG

Being Human

Fat, sloppy, ugly, nasty, retarded, stupid, loser, crazy, weird, liar, thief, devil . . .

I don't want to be any of these things. I want to be happy and liked by people. I'm not half of the things people call me. People probably don't know or see it, but I am a nice girl who cares about people. I don't like how people pick on people and put them down, especially when people do it to them and they don't like it, but they do it to others. I feel that if you don't like what people do to you, then you shouldn't do it to others. You don't have to like those people, but don't put them down—they are human. If you like them or not, treat them with respect. You probably don't notice or don't care, but it hurts a lot of people when you put them down or pick on them. So please don't, and remember that we are all human and that we all have feelings.

I sit here and wonder what is normal? I'm sure I got put in jail and police cars for being someone I'm not—people need to realize that I'm hurting because of what I've done.

STEPHANIE

༄

Body Talk

Feed me, soothe me, wash me
let me lay in the sun
you should probably go for a run
I feel like escaping,
let's have some fun

Be quiet a moment,
you petulant child!
Let me think, let me breathe
you are driving me wild!

You are too skinny,
you are too fat
your hair is too frizzy,
now what's up with that?!

Brown eyes are okay
if you just want to see,
but green eyes are pretty,
particularly

My bottom's too flat
and my belly too round
If only they could trade places,
like lost children now found

I want to eat cheeseburgers
laying in bed,
when what I know I need
is veggies instead

Demands from the outside,
demands from within
like all of my problems
will be solved when I'm thin

My body goes slowly while
my mind screams, "go fast"
This push and this pull
just can't possibly last

There's what I want, what I need,
and then in between
A photograph taken
from a messed-up crime scene

My body's my ally one day
and the next we're at war
Maybe I should just stop,
pause, and wonder
what's this fight really for?

JILL

When I Look in the Mirror

I see blue eyes so bright.
I see a lost soul.
Someone who criticizes herself too much.
Someone who's working hard on changing daily.
My mother staring back at me.
Guilt and shame.
Infinite potential.
Someone who wants to stay clean and sober.
A good friend. Not someone perfect,
but someone working on loving herself, and being
    the best she can be!

JOELLEN

To Be a Flower

Imagine how simple life would be and how many chances you would have; every year you get to start fresh. I guess that's kinda what my life has been like. Every time I'm released from prison, I start over from square one. Only I hold history and memories from the past. Do flowers hold history, do they remember?

STACY

Not Done Trying What I'll Be

Trying to be what I am not—
it's the only hope for the life I've got.
It takes away the stories that other people have
     often sought.
They didn't want the truth.
They didn't care to hear my plan.
I don't think they were capable to let me think "I
     can."
They always tell me "no."
When I try to stay, they tell me "go."
When I say I must go, that's in their control also.
So I will do my time in jail
to some it means I fail.
If they could see what I can see,
they'd see I'd won.
Go to hell, my ship's a-sail.
I have to work 'cause I get up in pain,
it's hard I know, I shouldn't complain.
When I go all out, it's strength I gain,
it makes my heart know why I came.
It will be a long time,
I got another record on my list of crimes,
but it will be over and then it will be fine.
'Cause I'll stick out my thumb where I go,
then the choice will be mine.

                                            ANGIE

My Heart's Craving

My heart craves to just walk off your opinions, let them fall to the ground and crumble under my feet. To not display the imprints of your anger on my skin.
My heart craves a cleansing rain to wash out what you told me I'd be, so that I can be me.

SUZANNE

Trying to Birth My Adult Self

Six years of empty time trying to find myself, trying to birth this so-called adult version of myself . . . through time we can become anyone. I've become everyone else's version of self . . . And I've yet to birth "the me" I'd like to be. Six years of labor . . . only to have an emergency C-section . . . Ripped out of the version of myself. Violently and unwillingly. I wasn't ready to meet the world as anybody, not me, not the adult version, not any version of me. Six years to realize my whole life was built on a foundation of lies. Six years only to recede back to those lies . . .

As violently as I was ripped from the womb, I'm being forced back in, forced to recreate myself. To "their" standards . . . All the regurgitation, all the sorting and organizing of feelings. Resentments harden. Never mattered. Small pieces in a much larger puzzle. I was never given all the pieces . . . my puzzle has been incomplete since birth . . .

To fail or succeed, I don't know what's worse. I'm forced to endure harsh truths and soft lies. My chest is full of rage. My womb, full of hate. Self-hatred, then hate on a much larger scale. I'm broken, but not in a good way, not in a conformity way; in a "fuck everyone" way, in the "fuck myself" way. In the "watch me rebirth a monster of myself" way . . . If six years didn't change me for the better, how much more time will it take before "they" realize time ain't the answer . . . I don't want the world to meet the monster in me . . . The monster six years in labor created . . . I wonder what lies "they" live . . . It took more than me to create this monster . . . The seed was in me, but they fertilized it . . . Lies kept it in my womb . . . While the truth nurtured her and watched her grow . . . Blind silent rage fed her . . .

STACY

Thanksgiving Feather

Opened door, coats taken and hung; so many it becomes a balancing act, an architectural puzzle of how to fit them all on the rack. Hugs all around, eight aunts, eight uncles, thirty–something cousins; *hellos, how are you's, what have you been up to's.*

Hors d'oeuvres set out, wine bottles opened, beers cracked, children scattering around the yard. Tables set, dishes heated, the laughter and chatter and cheer from the game on the wide screen

And then comes the time to set for dinner—but first our tradition, the most important of family traditions: the construction paper turkey where we each receive a feather to write what it is we are grateful for.

Then before we begin our feast, we each receive another's feather, read it aloud and try to guess who wrote what. I always used to dread the cheesy feather game thinking *"only my family," "we're lunatics," "how embarrassing."* But now that is what I am most grateful for . . . the symphonic chaos of our clan, the unorchestrated dance in the kitchen, the unconditional love, the feast; and yes even the feather.

JILL

Sadness

Sadness is wandering aimlessly down the long dark, damp path that leads nowhere; it just goes on and on without end. The tall trees with their bark peeling in long drooping tattered strips huddle so tightly together, no light could ever pierce through their leafy boughs. The ferns on the damp mildewy forest floor are withering a slow painful death; their leaves brown and brittle curl inward as if in the fetal position. The shadows seem to follow Sadness, waiting for just the right moment to swallow Her up in their dark outstretched folds. If only they could comfort her tortured soul, she would gladly succumb. No love can be found in the dark shadows, so on and on Sadness travels, hoping to one day see the light.

NORAJEAN

Dance in the Rain

I am waiting for Prince Charming to come swooping in, pick me up and carry me away to a far-away land where I can live happily ever after . . . In that land, nobody knows of sadness, hurt, anger, deceit or hate. Here, those types of emotions do not exist. Here, you simply live to love, with only what you have to give from your heart. Complete affection and care for one another. An unspeakable zest for life that nothing can overcome. The days are filled with laughter. Honesty lives on the tip of our tongues. The sun shines bright and warm in the sky. There is never darkness. But wait . . .

Isn't this the way the earth was first created to be? Then how did it become so desolate? How come everybody turns their backs on one another? Either live in the why every day wondering what's gone wrong; or learn to dance in the rain, skate through the sleet, swim through the tide and know that through every heartache and every tear, you learn a little and become that much stronger.

MELISSA G

Darkness and Truth

Truth is blurred somewhere in time, somewhere between the lines. Truth fades when you don't look it in the eyes. It's easy to forget, to give in to simple lies. If I speak truth, I have to like regret, throw up shame, accept resentment, feel bitter in my blood stream. I would rather avoid truth than look me in my eyes to see who I've become. I feel her presence within me. She is out for self. She has no loyalty and knows no love. Anger drives her. Revenge brings a sparkle to her eye. You can almost see the smile there.

I look in her eyes. I turn my head out of fear. Is that really me in there? Those angry bitter eyes. Chest tight. Truth heavy. Hate is harder, more loyal than love. Rage in my chest. Lies in my stomach. Spite in my mouth. Truth in my heart. I'm at war with my self. But she is winning, consuming me, forcing me to be everything I hated.

No more light. No more faith. Just darkness and truth . . . No more lies to string me along. Just pain, self-inflicted wounds. I was mad at her, I was mad at the world. I blamed him, I blamed them. But it's me. I hate me. Maybe I blame me too much.

When did I become weak? When did I give in? When did I start to believe that rage and resentment would carry me home? When did I become so sick? Why can't I turn back? Truth is, history is ingrained in me, forcing me to see it: us against them, me against the world. Alone. Angry. Bitter. Harder than I should be 'cuz I'm forced to be. And maybe it wasn't just my choices. 'Cuz I still hear their voices.

Stacy

Just When I Believe I'm Gone

A deep pounding drum beats in my head, pain rippling with each strike, keeping time to the storm gathering strength within my dark exhausted soul.

It picks up speed, whirling swiftly in my stomach now.

Despair and hopelessness are angrily dancing to the drum, while clouds erupt, rain mixed with salty tears densely falling like a veil, shielding and protecting me, a small child crouched and hiding from all of this, from this storm and ultimately, the resulting erosion of self . . . gritty and sandy remains, dirty and muddy, not pretty or easy to deal with . . .

I unfold myself, reaching and striving for I know this is real and I must simply go through these unpleasant emotions and face my realities.

Rampant destruction remains . . . How can I fix anything? No success left to be had . . . bright orange-red flames are now licking the surface, burning through what is left here, the dark contours of my desolate soul . . . Fire awakening pain, pain allows healing . . .

For if the pain has always been beneath layers and layers of other landscapes, how can it ever be felt, dealt with, and finally dissipated?

Pain's veins branch out, expanding so far until they reach every inch of my body and soul, even visible under a tentative smile or love that is co-existing . . .

The fire is now burning within my mind, body and soul at this point. I am in pain's clutches, he holds me in his huge hands, threatening to swallow me whole never to be again . . .

Just when I believe I'm gone and I'm begging for mercy, I am yanked out to find a beautiful bright new place exists underneath it all. Pain has died, for now, and the messy life has been cleansed by rain, and then christened by fire leaving me to start anew.

Tiffany H

If I Was Home

As I sit here by my barred window, all I can do is think what the world is doing tonight? With the sky clear and a couple of stars in it. I know what I would be doing if I was home with my family. We would all be cuddled up on my bed with a big bowl of popcorn watching Halloween movies together. Then after watching movies, I would have the children go to bed and I would clean up; and then I would go and give them kisses and tuck them into bed and say a prayer.

As I would walk out of the empty rooms where my children used to be, I would break down and cry; 'cause now someone else is kissing them and putting them to bed. Why can't it be me? Then I remember I will always be with them in blood and heart and soul; 'cause they are my blood, heart and soul, all in one.

TH

Jailed

Jail—
the place nobody wants to be.
Bail—
the only way to get free.

Crawling through the underbrush of my life,
the air is ripe with hate;
looks can cut like a knife.
This is my fate.

Just like Vietnam
the enemy's all around.
I'm like a ticking bomb;
shush, don't make a sound.

Creeping silently about
trying not to be heard;
there should be no doubt
thinking there's no danger is absurd.

Jailed—
it's like an insidious disease.
Nailed—
sneaks up on you, brings you to your knees.

ELAINA

Tracing Myself

See my face for the second time.
Dark. Darkness. Night. No light.
No rewind.
No redo.
No step back.
Stop . . . The End.

A second chance . . . why?

Open my eyes. I can't talk.
  I can't walk
  I can't see
  I can't be
  I don't want to be

Where am I?
  I don't know
  I don't want to know

Who am I?
  I don't know anymore
  I want to know who
  I am now
  I can't see me
  in the mirror
  I don't want to

"Put on some eyeliner, you're going to feel better,"
  they told me.
I can't. Don't want to. I want to see me, Louise,
  again.
So do it, put some eyeliner on, it's going to trace
  yourself.

LOUISE

My Canvas, My Song

I feel freed from reality, free to let my thoughts and imagination flow here on these pages, free to express myself at will and whim, to write of fairy tales and long-lost places, of memories and long-lost faces. Whimsical and carefree, my pen glides smoothly along, bringing out of my soul all that lives there in the depths, the laughter and love, the heartache and pain, reality and fantasy. Letters and words fall into their places, as easy as the stars twinkle in space, forming on the page to see, a story that is all about me. This is my canvas, this is my song. The words are my freedom, there is no right or wrong. Here in this world of words, I feel I belong.

NORAJEAN

I Can't Just Let It Go

"Do you hear voices?"

"Yes."

"Do you see people or things others can't see?"

"Yes."

"What do they say? What do you see?"

"They're scary, but not at first. They look kind and friendly. Comforting as can be. They say they'll be my friend or take care of me. Then, as it progresses, everything progressively starts to change. They turn into monsters and then I know they're evil and want to take my soul from me."

"Why don't you relax? Don't worry so! You'd feel so much better if you'd just let it go."

It's always the same. I cry in shame. I'm a joke and excuse for others to bitch. The resentments and worries are what people see and profess and describe me. Again I'm the ass, and it's stuck in my heart and mind and torments me.

There's so many people both inside and out and they all got big mouths without a doubt. Then there's the little of me that is real. Some people get to know a part most don't see. Experience things I still enjoy and sometimes get to share. I get to show I'm human and make them aware.

ANGIE

What If

What if you woke up and weren't where you went to sleep? What if somehow, our world was changed overnight? What if we could go home better people than we were when we arrived? I hope I will be. I hope that when I leave, things will be easier, more organized and less dependent on me. What if the religion that controls my Mother's mind were to decide it was OK to be me? What if I finally got on the right meds . . . Would I be "normal," would I hurt or wonder if I were doing it right so much?

If I got this straightened out, would l feel like I was worth taking care of, too: or would I still spend all my time caring for others? Would I find out that this is normal, and I am different for wanting it to be different? What if we woke up and found we were the crazy ones and the rest of the world was right all along? I fear this, I don't wish it.

MICHELE

Artwork by Norajean

More Life Than Stillness

I hold myself here
   tense, pensive, and
     waiting.
My world is
razor wire and bars
   guards and
     cold-hearted steel.

This life within me
   is quieter each day
smothered by the
   total disregard for
     others.

I drown in falsehoods,
   begging, for what
     I don't know . . .

Time? Freedom?
Loyalty and Truth?
I would settle for
   Friendship
     if only I could find it.

MARGARITA

Power in Silence

If I don't tell, no one will ever know.
Therefore, I can hold and own that power.
The knowledge of the experience is mine alone.
The choice to hold it in or to express it to someone
    else is another source of my power.
Power in silence.
Power in choice.
My Power. Unfamiliar!
Rare for me to feel powerful in silence.
If the silence is my choice, I can turn that into a
    source of strength.
To feel strong on the inside, to have an inner voice,
    an inner choice.
My voice.
My choice.
My strength.

No one can take my knowledge away from me,
    copy it or steal it.
I don't have to share it.
Not now, not ever.
And so it's a part of me forever.

HEATHER

⌒ᕙ

Unspoken Words

At night I lay in bed
with words unspoken
drowning my head.
I think of how to express my feelings,
but all my words turn into Demons.
I know if I hold all the words within
a world of horror will soon begin.
Keeping it all bottled up
eyes filled with tears swelling
full of these unspoken words
full of the unspoken pain,
full of the unspoken guilt.
If my words stay unspoken
will I ever feel whole again?
No.
Will he ever forgive me
or look past my faults?
Probably not.
Soon these words will be forgotten,
like bad fruit, rotten.
Now I lay to go to sleep
with unspoken words haunting
my dreams.

KAYLA

Patience

If you listen to the ringing in your ears, your heart racing as your mind says quicker, quicker, quicker . . . go, go, go, yet your body yearns for solitude, and "patience" seems like a foreign word . . . waiting at the end of the line having to sit and think about the life you left behind . . . not knowing when or if you'll get back in time . . . listening to the radio, waiting for your favorite song to play. Day turns to night, and it never played . . . not having the choice to change the disc or skip the CD . . . waiting for the great day to come when you will hear good news. Maybe you can get back to your life and your own choices. Now you've waited and waited long enough and what they call "patience" is all you have left inside your hurting soul . . . having no choice but to endure this complicated situation you've put yourself in . . . being left with no choice but to be patient. God knows that once you lose patience, the consequences will only hurt worse and steal more light from your already aching soul. Some say "patience is a virtue." Yet, I must ask, is it a virtue or a necessary tool for this place we call "life"?

BE

Legacy of Regret

The truth is, the future only lies ahead for a few of us today. For many, our future only holds the past. I know. Until a few months ago, the past had a choking grip on everything I wanted to be. The past told me who I could be, who I could love . . . and who I should hate. I never questioned it; just thought that that was the way it was supposed to be. And then something strange happened. I lied. I became someone else, and by doing that I learned who I could be.

You see, I thought that by telling a lie I could change one person, change a whole family—maybe the future. But a lie is never a good foundation for the future. It crumbles when you least expect it. I learned that I can't change people through lies. The truth is, I can't change people at all. There is only one thing that I know for sure that I can change—and that's me.

So don't let your past strangle you. Will you look back ten, fifteen . . . twenty years from now and regret the person that you've become? Will you look back and wonder what could have been? If you look back with regret, you have no one to blame but yourself, because legacies don't hold on to you, you hold on to them. We all have the power to move on. Don't let mistakes or legacies smother your dreams. Go after them . . . because regret makes a very bitter traveling companion.

DANA

Birthday Inside Concrete Walls

I will celebrate my birthday inside this year, inside concrete walls painted pastel, egg-shell colors. I will open no presents and blow out no candles. In fact, I will most probably choose to let the day pass like any other.

But I will celebrate because I know, I *know* that past the covered windows, the fence with razor wire, past the locked doors and steel cages, I am not alone. I will close my eyes and picture the faces that I know will take a moment on this day to send their love through a thought, a spark, a desire to remember . . .

And it is then that I will celebrate images held, lips curved upward, a small laugh followed by a gentle tear. Another year, I will be boundless right here within these walls. So on this (birth)day, when you see me walking down the hall, mop in hand, broom to sweep, but it looks something different, like I'm not here . . .

Don't you see? I'm not here at all, I am finally free, because him, her, and him are on the outside blowing candles out for me.

JILL

To Be Silent

To be silent is to be alone, not seen, not heard,
unknown;
to be silent is to feed into your fears. But what if
your fears are justified?
If I say, "this will happen," will it happen for sure;
or is it just a strong possibility?
Is there any possibility something good will happen
if you are heard?
I say YES!
Can you live with yourself knowing you let something good go by being silent?
If not, don't speak; if yes, should I speak?
Don't just think before you speak; think before you
are silent.

MICHAELA

Leaning Out and Listening

I was leaning out, I was listening
to every word you said.
I was trying so hard to accomplish everything
that I leaned too far, and fell instead.
And yet and still, it was told to me
the things I needed to know:
I led my mind with my heart
and continued to damage my soul.

I hit rock bottom,
still the voice asked me to listen;
and in me doing so,
I knew that I was forgiven.

I could have sworn I had the answers;
I could have sworn I'd be so right.
Yet my world came tumbling down
every day and night.
So I found a solution; I finally realized
that everything I was listening to
was also right before my eyes.
It was told from the beginning
I just had to read between the lines,
take a better look at things
without being mesmerized.

It wasn't that I couldn't understand—
the voice made it very clear;
it wasn't that I needed a helping hand,
because I had no fear.
You see, indeed I was listening
but I just couldn't hear!

JOSEPHINE

I've Been Known . . .

I've been known to say the first thing that pops into my head with little care for how it will be received by the listener. I've been known to say things aggressively, leaving no doubt that I meant what I had said, almost like a bully trying to force my will on my listener. A bully on the outside, a scared quivering bowl of Jello on the inside, afraid they will see through my protection—my words—to the frightened child within afraid of not being accepted.

I've been known to say some comforting words, words that can wrap themselves around my listeners, enveloping them with their warmth and compassion. These words, although from my mouth, I believe are from the Holy Spirit working through me. And then, and only then, I have been known to be still and just feel the warmth that surrounds me always.

. . . to Just Be.

NORAJEAN

You Don't Know Me

I imagine others will think or better yet, won't really know what to think when and if they are given the opportunity to get to know me—the real me. I don't grant such invitations to very many people; so if I do, it is because I felt respected and that you were trustworthy and special enough to understand me and love me for who I truly am.

Who I am on the inside doesn't always show on the outside, especially when I'm in this concrete jungle, and we are stripped from our clothes and jewelry and stuck into lovely uniforms. Some days I'd even be happy to wear my grandmother's polyester instead of the blues. They want us all to be the same—Good Luck! They can strip our outer beings, but then in order to be individuals, our personalities, mannerisms, voices, talents beliefs and actions become more prominent.

At a glance you'd think I am quiet, shy, and a goody two-shoes . . . ha! ha! To me and those who know me, I am the farthest from all of that. In here it is hard for me to show who I am. I've had some bad experiences and as much as I'd love to be the out-going happy-go-lucky girl I am out on the streets, I shut down in here.

DANA

Freedom Rider: An Advertisement

Woman of fifty actual years, give or take plus or minus from that reference point, depending entirely upon maturity level of that particular day, although subject to change at the drop of a hat. Actually quite tall if you could ever glimpse her in the rare moment that she is standing. Usually known by the jazzy, candy apple red scooter she buzzes around in. You know, the one with the "caution—wide load" sign flashing from the rear? Her salt-and-pepper hair either streaming out behind her as she goes or knocked askew by the many writing utensils poking out here and there (never remembered when one is needed, however).

Her little dog riding excitedly on one of her legs eagerly helping to chase down her mind that is running ahead like mad, its fuzzy blue slippers flapping and swapping on the ground as it seeks a safer haven. If you should see this oddity pass you by, quickly jump out of the way. This slightly cracked child of God, although not meaning to, will definitely run over your toes.

NORAJEAN

~

The Truth Within

The truth within me is very unbalanced. Some days I'm even emotionless and even scared. I'm scared of not being this perfect person that my community wants. But I just want to be me and free of my past and to move on with a great future in front of me, one with love of family and for myself. Maybe even be open to a relationship of tender heart. To get rid of being scared that my past will come out. I am who I am. And all that matters is that I feel free of the past and I've moved on to a brighter future.

MG

~

Reading Scars

Those of us who survive here
by reading scars,
finding faults
before they open up and swallow us

talk gingerly. We learned early
to whisper, tiptoe, skirt
our way around.

We live by losing
love by letting go
enduring the random uprooting.
We drown in downpours.

Because we find ourselves so often
unable to speak
endings without stories,
scattered notes instead of songs,
what will it take?

Will my children tell whole stories?
Will they dance?
Will they be able to push down
beyond the scars and faults?
Oh, how I pray they be filled
with a sense of their own
belonging, to be fruit
undamaged.

NORAJEAN

Chased by Demons

Trapped inside of my own mind,
seeing myself as one of a kind.
Dark skies swirling high above,
the world, lacking beauty and love.

Running fast from the demons,
chasing me, they are scheming.
Pushing my way through the dark,
the air is cold and stark.

Wondering if there is anyone out there,
anyone left that truly cares.
Knowing that I am being caught,
caught up by the demons I brought.

I must have asked for them to come;
I was blind when I wanted them.
Going round and round in the blackness,
just creating a bigger mess.

How do I shake the dark around me
so thick and heavy I can't see;
dropping down on the ground,
seeking for what must be found.

My head heavy in my hands
seeking for a means to an end,
tears streaming down my face.
Is this my final place?

Screaming what is meant to be,
realizing I have been chasing me.

RAVEN

Breaking Free

To be in this world means to suffer. If you learn from that, making yourself stronger and smarter, you become a soldier. A brave courageous person who protects what they believe in. Breaking free from the walls built to protect the body while locking in the soul. There is nothing that can destroy a person worse than seeing what they've believed in has no value; and worse, is proven to be a lie. It will ruin the whole person's being. They will become a sad, lost soul searching for a new goal. Blessed are those who recognize that, as their lives are falling apart, they are given the ability, through guidance, to repair life before there's nothing left.

MELISSA G

While Beauty Remains

Beauty, what is it really?

A soft rose petal against the roughness of your lover's cheek.

The struggle of memories of being younger when you get older.

The sharpness of a razor against a smooth leg.

The long wait of a fortune, a nail the length of the table for a heart attack.

Muscle failure for fitting into a nice pair of jeans.

Track marks for a good nod.

Jail time for a piece of the pie.

Rehab for all the great parties attended.

Prison for that one drink that killed your best friend.

Scars for the fast life.

Tattoos for growing old both saggy and God knows what.

Death for being brought into this life.

Loved for hating so much.

Living the devil's way 'til God intervenes and takes you away.

Good looks for bad attitude.

A loving family for you even though you left them behind.

Kids that love you that you've abandoned.

The beauty for me is to be set free from this life I've chosen to walk.

Before there is no beauty left in me.

FLIP

Chaos Came Calling

The guest that visited me today was Chaos. My usual schedule was disrupted. I had no work crew today. So I skipped breakfast and slept in. I got up for lunch and as soon as I came back to the unit from lunch, "he" was here. Chaos, I mean. He whispered in my ear in the bathroom and then called me to the officer's desk and told me I would be moving to another room.

Chaos knows that loud things are my trigger, and loud arguments can send me scurrying under my bed, covering my ears and humming to cover it up. Chaos gave me the opportunity to do just that. I, however, being grown up on the outside, just sat on the bed and plugged my ears.

After the loudness and arguments were over, I stayed in my room. I am afraid I was not a good hostess for Chaos. I didn't offer him a drink or ask him to sit and stay. Chaos is a guest I don't really care for. I wish Chaos would never visit or that I knew better how to deal with Chaos as a visitor. Maybe there is a class?

MICHELE

I Am Waiting . . .

for Saturday to see my loving children who I haven't seen for almost four years. I am waiting to hold them, touch them and smell them; see their changes—height, weight, hair, eyes, smiles, their being; spend as much time in my two hours of catch-up as I can, for I don't know when I will see them again.

I am waiting for them, longing for them. I feel numb waiting for them. Is it true? Will it really come?? I am waiting to see them, and watch them, and remember them 'til I see them again.

I am waiting so nervously, afraid, worried yet happy, emotional and feeling kind of empty. I think, where do I belong, where do I go from here, how long will I be waiting again; and I wonder, will they be able to wait with me, waiting to see, feel, smell me?

I am waiting for them.

DEB

Four O'clock in the Morning

It comes lapping at me like I've only just closed my eyes, but there I am beginning my day again. I lay solid like a rock in my bed, listening to movement, grounding myself, preparing my mind for work and playing a quick game of dress as quick as you can, under cold room temperatures.

The room goes silent as I shut off the fan. Here comes my day. Brush the teeth, doing the hygiene thing. Rush to wait at the several doors I must go through to get to work. Ahh, I've made it. It's 4 a.m. and I'm here, have shown up for another day at this kitchen to try and navigate my path, and to try and smooth out any ruffled feathers that might arise from being at work so early without the adequate amount of coffee to deal with people's slower minds. And I quickly flex my muscles and get to work trying to push past 8 a.m. My work is done. Amen.

TESS

I Wish I Was Closer to Home

I am in solitary here.
The only guests I see are the ones who choose to
  come.
I wish I was closer to home.
Here I feel so alone.
My celly is my permanent guest.
We treat each other honorably, for we have to live
  with one another.
We have become close.
We stand to one another.
I wish I was closer to home.
I wish I was home where the ones I want close to
  me I do not consider guests—my loved one, my
  children, my spouse, friends, family.
Where happiness is common and not just a guest
  who comes and goes.
I wish I was home.

KAYLA

Life "Inside"

Caged like animals at the zoo
being watched, on display.
The guards know all that we do
all through the night and day.

Sometimes it feels almost as though
we're here for their amusement.
Creatures milling to and fro,
none of us are heaven sent.

They watch us sleep,
they hear us roar.

Just our thoughts they can't keep;
life isn't what it was before.

We have to watch what we say,
be careful what we do.
There are times when we play
but, usually, we're feeling blue.

We make a friend,
we socialize;
but in the end,
no one hears us cry.

We're in a crowd
but so all alone.
Sometimes we get loud
when we bitch and moan.

We eat bad food,
take their medication.
We sit and brood,
wishing for probation.

We aspire to greatness
but we fall just short.
We often give much less
when we're out of sorts.

We live on what we're given
but it's not very much.
It's not really living
when you use others as a crutch.

We're left with just our souls,
which can truly fly free.
We all have our goals.
We all have our dreams.

Elaina

Stopping Chaos

This time away has been incredibly tough. Not without sorrow, sadness and many tears. Lost without my children, my husband, my life. Guilty for my sins, dedicating myself to the work on my sobriety. I don't want to be here anymore, or again. Praying for a second chance, that things will be different, that I will be different. That it won't be so difficult to keep my head clear of the chaos, because when the chaos starts, it's usually not good and once it starts, I don't know how to stop it. So I'm dedicating myself to learning how to stop the chaos.

MH

Coiled Spring

I feel like folding back on myself,
coiled up like a spring. Becoming tenser,
tighter, edgier. Tenser, tighter, edgier.
TENSER, TIGHTER, EDGIER . . . *SNAP!!*
I spring forward, I run . . . where?
I don't know. I just know to stay here is death.
To stay here is to be a rotting corpse.
So I run. I run to be free. I run to see.
I run to see the truth. The truth is
I long to be free. Not the freedom that comes
from being let out of jail. I long for the freedom
from the imprisonment of my own mind
The worst and most tortuous place for me to be.
The heavy chains of past guilt. Real or imagined.
Past wrongs of varying degrees. I am the worst
    judge,
jury, jailor. So I run to be free.
But . . . how?

BILLIE

Companions

Booze and lies put me in
    this place.
Now, I find I need a time-
    out
before I can show my face,
of this I have no doubt.

Shame and guilt over-
    whelm me,
anger is always at my side.
This is no way for life to
    be,
I feel something within me
    has died.

There's always hatred,
my second best friend,
through him a lot has been
    said,
there's so much I can't
    mend.

I can't forget my buddy,
    pain,
always under the surface,
whenever I feel any strain,
he's always on my case.

Sometimes it's regret that's
    there,
always butting his way in.
Together we're a lovely
    pair,
both of us are as guilty as
    sin.

ELAINA

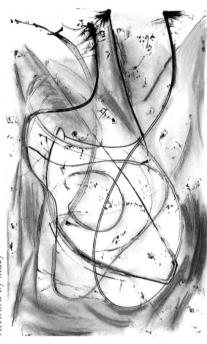

Artwork by Stacy

The Fast Life

The fast life—cars, people, bright lights—does it ever stop, or slow down to take time to gather its thoughts? Does it tell the truth; or does it forget what it has said? I can run away in this fast life and be lost in my world, and its world of non-stopping, always moving, looking over my shoulder to make sure my lies are not following. Then, when the parties crash and the lights flicker and the cars stop, life comes to a reality. It hits me all at once.

The fact is that I am not out there in that fast life; I am sitting here in this cell all by myself wishing I was out there with my family. The fact is that life's not fast right now and I am not in that bright light or those cars. Reality is life's hard. I've had a few crashes that I am trying to break out of, and be on the right lane with the right people, with the right lights. This is my life, slowly coming along.

CZ

Choices

The wind blows across the sands of time, eternally shifting, rolling, changing from a slope here, a wave there; reminding us how quickly and easily our lives can be changed, a door can be opened between right and wrong. We have but to step through; what direction shall we go? A cry of warning echoes deep within: *shall I walk the path to the heavens or lie lost in the land of thirst, parched and bound by the twisted vines, strangling my true nature, to become forever changed—and not for the better?*

NORAJEAN

Test of Faith

This week has been the worst rollercoaster of my life, finding out the most wonderful news and then hit with the worst ever. A true test of faith. The only explanation is answer to prayers that I and others have made. So from this miracle I have decided to not second-guess my belief; to get into the Word, rely on the one and only who is there for us always. Remembering we are only given what we need, not what we want. Remembering that once you have prayed upon your need, praise Him.

Federal Inmate. Court cancelled. Court—attorney meetings—marshalls—transport—court—lawyer meeting cancelled—staying through 'til Monday—child visit Saturday night and perhaps a special visit with oldest daughter and grandchildren. Only a power greater than authority. Manifested through my belief.

DEB

Dedication to Tranquility

In this environment it takes a great deal of commitment to dedicate yourself to tranquility of inner spirit. I am trying to learn how to become more aware of self; how my actions and reactions affect others.

I awake each morning nurturing my body with yoga for its overall health and well-being throughout the day. There was a couple of months that I was over-eating due to my emotions. I am trying to commit to eating more healthy now.

As of today, I am going to be more dedicated to not giving my power away to others. I often find that in this environment, certain situations that are repetitive with the same people can be reminders of your upbringing and can trigger responses without even a reaction time.

I dedicate myself today to meditate longer and honor my personal integrity. I feel as though I have been losing that.

TONYA

Moments Like These

I hate the feeling of having to need anybody. Period. Let alone for support, such as a conversation or letter. Seems like such simple things to ask for, yet so hard for one to receive.

I miss my life, my independence, my freedom, my self-esteem. People who are institutionalized may listen to me and say, *"aaaah, deal with it and suck it up."* But it's moments like these that I'd like to keep in mind. For if I intended to do something that were to jeopardize my freedom, I'll look back and relive this very moment of feeling such hopelessness, such unconfident, uncontrollable feelings of powerlessness and misery. And do everything in my power not to have to actually go through moments like these.

JOSEPHINE

Tree That Took My Life

My roots have planted deep over the past three years as I watched this tree branch out into so many directions, the trunk heavy with despair. My soul would become so happy if it could just let down over another broken branch. I have fallen slave to the devil's horns again: cocaine, my best friend. Helps to ease the pain of the day I fell asleep and drove into a family friend. Now he lives, but has no way to fend.

Another branch broke today. I violated conditions after coming home from Virginia. Into jail I go. Four years this time. This is where I belong, I know. My favorite place is my internal shame chamber that I never, never have to leave. The branches always stay nice and strong for me.

I've been home now for quite some time triggered by every sound or noise. Each anniversary I may fall off the highest branch. But the bang when I hit the bottom always feels good. At the end of this year, I am maxing out my sentence with the angry rent-a-roos, leaving behind the razor wire and waving goodbye to ice island forever—right after I chop down this tree that took my life. Now I am ready to create my tree of life.

TONYA

Just One More Day

Depression and despair
nipping at my heels.
No one around to care
about how it really feels.

Exiled from society
thrown behind locked, steel doors
I ask "why is this happening to me"
as I pace these cold tiled floors.

I try to tell myself
"Just one more day,"
for my own mental health
it has to be that way.

Time can heal old wounds,
but man can't speed up time.
It's like being on an island; marooned,
all because of just one crime.

The stress is getting to me,
breaking through my protective shell.
Everyone here would agree,
this is their own private hell.

Happy thoughts don't exist,
prayers being said
blue eyes filled with mist
crazy thoughts in my head.

No one cares, nor do they know
exactly how I feel.
I have no friends, only foes,
in this place, so unreal.

ELAINA

No One to Call

I have difficulty being on the phones here. My only contact left is with my father who would rather sit in companionable silences than hold a conversation. When I used to talk to my Joe, we used songs to convey the feelings that we didn't want others to know about. We had "our song" which would sound obvious to some and not so to others. My mother doesn't speak to me on the phone unless there is no one else home. And I have no phone numbers for either my nineteen-year-old son or my twenty-one-year-old daughter. Losing my Joe basically lost my phone privileges because without him I no longer have anyone to call.

I always raced for the phone when I was younger. It would never be for me, but I always wanted to answer it. After several years of answering phones for different companies, the excitement went out of it and dread took its place. "Oh, God, not another creditor," I'd think. "They are gonna want me to promise them something, and I can't do that. Even if the boss lets me promise them something, he won't let me follow through on the promise." So when the phone rang, I would take a deep breath and prepare to either lie or pretend I was a secretary who knew nothing. I got good at both of those falsehoods at my last job.

MICHELE

Unwanted Answers

Every time I pick up the phone I get answers, but not the answers I want. However, I always get the answer I expected. Lately it's become a let-down and it makes me feel even worse, not only stressed and depressed, but alone, abandoned, and betrayed all at once. My mother will always be a mother, and speak the truth about reality; but that's something I can't bear to hear all the time. Now I'm always in a dreadful and depressing mood every time I get hold of that phone. My mother always told me, "TRUST NO ONE." And trusting less than a handful got me here, so now I understand. To my knowledge now—you don't know what you don't have until you're gone; and when you're gone, what you have is simply the truth.

JOSEPHINE

Repeat, Repeat, Repeat

10 a.m., no answer.
Is he sleeping?
3 p.m. Still sleeping?
or maybe cheating?
My mind races
try again and again.
It's clockwork.
Finally at 10 p.m.
he answers
nothing but repeat
supposedly sleeping?
silence
me screaming.
Now I'm on checks
possibly suicidal
nah, more like homicidal!
I hate him!
OK, I let it go;
wake up;
it's my repeat,
call again and again
with nothing to end up
besides crying again and again
to do nothing but care again.
To do nothing but repeat
what I know I share
not care to begin with!
But that's me, just repeat, repeat, repeat.

KH (DECEASED 2012)

Dreamscape

I want to land on my feet this time, and not feel bad or cry any more. I always wonder when my feet will bring me home. I have the same dreams every night. Everything I had goes up in smoke,

and it will always be going up and up and up.

JESS

You and Me, Son

Before I know it, you will be all grown up. Where has time gone? Where has the past gone? I know where . . . on dumb times partying and not paying attention to you. Why do we fuck up so bad? 'Cause we do not see what we have in front of us until it is too late. Sorry for all that. It is time to be there. As soon as I get out of jail, it's you and me, son, no one else—we need to have fun.

BELINDA

Corner of Loneliness

"Please try your call again later." Sighing, I hang the plastic black receiver up and continue staring at the numbers on the keypad. You never seem to be on the other end anymore . . . The guard hands out stacks of cards and letters. As usual, I receive nothing.

I am here.
Alone.
Forgotten.
Buried in pain.

My mind turns the corner of loneliness, extracting hope as if with a tiny syringe, sucking it in from my soul and injecting it into my current state. Bright red, pungent, stinging my veins. It hurts to hope because you never come. You never answer. You never write.

And yet, I magically produce more, even now, as snow lightly decorates the ground; even as December marches on in pageantry and decoration. You are mine and I am yours. We always say we are family, and family NEVER LEAVES family!

But you're gone.

The concept fails to compute on even the most primitive level in my gray, mushy brain. A movie plays out in my imagination . . . possibilities . . .

You and I, hands intertwined, blue eyes locked in chocolate brown ones, giggling while we drop to the ground making snow angels, arms frantically waving, brushing snow in that up-and-down flying motion, breath escaping as clouds dissipating in inky black night . . .

Or standing silently crying while the police cuffs my hands too tightly behind my back you watching me as you plead with the officers, begging them to let me have a cigarette, to be kind to me, to let me warm up under your oversized Adidas zip-up hoodie. They usher me out, and you follow the procession, crying and shouting to the world that you love, no matter what, unconditionally, before you disappear behind the door and I disappear down the road in the dusty, caged black-seat under my own salty tears, into dark, unknown oblivion . . .

TIFFANY H

Tuning Out Tempers

I heard when you stop looking at "*what's in it for me?*" you begin to see what's so important to the life that passes by. Today I was faced with many challenges and none of them were easy to get past. I found myself angry, embarrassed and feeling the outcast. I quietly spoke my mind, but it was like speaking with no voice; it whipped by their ears like it was the wind.

The yelling, angry words, hot tempers made me feel like I was back in the mixing pot of my addiction. Suddenly I felt afraid, non-trusting and alienated myself just to get a new perspective on how I was emotionally attached to my surroundings. I took deep breaths, relaxed my whole body and closed my eyes, trying to quiet my mind, slow down the race of thoughts, my heart and just be . . .

Grateful for where I am at in life and trying to figure out what's the purpose of this situation and how to move past it.

TESS

Mayhem

Utter, complete total chaos.
Everyone, with their two-second attention span,
blindfolded for words. I'm at a loss.
What a strange, cruel, ugly land . . .
people all riled up as if they're at some hillbilly mud-
    bog.
Girls zipping by, ricocheting into each other's rooms.
Nasty, unfeminine, acting like hogs!
Time to clean them up; Brillo pad, lava soap, tribase
    and brooms.
Finally—headcount. Quiet for now, I begin to think.
If they'd only take a daily twenty-minute walk,
maybe they'd be more lax, stop acting like such dinks.
Every day they watch you feels like they stalk you!
Survival of the fittest—I can make it. I can survive this.
Friend or foe? Who is which? How can I tell?
"No way out" Hotel California; all of this I'd never
    miss.
I am so sick of this place called hell.

VALERIE

Would I Always Live Like This?

Cement walls, the sound of mechanical locks opening doors that would slam shut behind me. Being told when to sleep and when to rise. Moving through the days like a robot. No emotion. Just being. Would I always live like this? Having no say in what to eat or when. What time to take medication. Having to force down drugs that have been crushed up and loaded into applesauce because we can't be trusted to take them whole. Would I always live like this? NO THANK YOU! What incentive to do the right things on the outside—that I never have to see these walls ever again. Would I always live like this? I think not! I don't want to be a robot.

Norajean

A Gift

You know, I love those cards you make . . .

Thank you!

My daughter's birthday is Sunday, she'll be eighteen. Do you think you could make one for her?

Sure; but I charge to make cards.

Oh. Sorry, I can't afford it. I have no money.

Oh, well, I'll make it for you anyway.

Are you sure?

Yes . . .

I sat down and made the card, thinking, *I don't have money either, that's why I'm making them, for the things I need while I'm here.*

I waited for her after I finished her card. Not even knowing her name.

As soon as I seen her, I told her, *Come with me, I have your card.* She was excited.

As I handed her the card, tears welled up in her eyes.

I love it; you know dragon flies are a sign of wisdom. And blue is her favorite color! You're gonna make me cry!

I said, *You're welcome,* as she walked away. I sat feeling emotional from her reaction to the beautiful card. I took in a deep breath and looked up. I could see her from where I was sitting.

She was leaning off her bed in her cell, holding the card. Just looking at it in admiration. Crying. Tears flowed down her cheeks and I took it in, thinking, she admires and appreciates something I dearly enjoy doing in life. And through that very art, we both embraced its property to heal.

TESS

Laughing from Inside

How barbaric of these officers to hold the women
from the sun which shines from the great blue sky.
It shines from within the soul when the laughter
    seeps by
these dungeons—or even Ice Islands
that hold so many women.
Stagnating laughter that should thrive
can't because the man holds
each and every one of us back.
Yet angry screams embedded in the cement
walls rage so deep it's buried in the foundation.
Those in charge of Razor Wire Inn
walk by these shrieks, hear these knocks, ignore
    the pleads
for healthier choices, of another chance for
daylight . . .
where laughter lies inside
daylight
where sunshine resides
peace subsides
looking around now, these women hold hands, feel
    free
laughing together. This is how prison should be
if only the officials would stand up and hear our
    cries;
but we laugh from the inside, we mustn't cry.

TONYA

Winding Road

A time or two in life, I've fallen;
the fall seems to go on and on.
It seems like forever,
like the speed of lightening.
I crash,
crashing so hard I hear the
snap and breaks of my bones.
The winding trail at ninety miles an hour
seemed like fun at the moment.
Until the blood seeped through
my cracked head.
Scars of a lifetime add up
to this very moment:
the wind in my hair, the abrupt stop
the flips
the stop
the pain
the end.

FLIP

Tough Love

Patience is not my strong suit. I've had to work diligently to acquire this most humble virtue. Patience did not run deep in my family either. So when it comes to my own patience, my only role models were priests, nuns, and school teachers—and that didn't run as deeply as you might think. I humbled myself with my conversations with God—He alone showed me that His will be done was what I had to accept in His, and only His own time.

I had major back surgery when I was fifteen years old. I convalesced in a full-body cast, flat on my back for six months. I had my first taste of my true human nature when all was taken from me so quickly. I lost my freedom. I lost my spirit. I gained humility and patience.

When I became a nurse in 1981 at just twenty-one, I learned that my patients didn't always tell time by my watch.

When I married at twenty-four, I didn't realize that husbands could also be as impatient as their wives.

When I went on to have three sons in quick succession, I had to really put on my thinking-cap to keep up with their demands and needs.

When I went to prison in 2004, I learned to wait for all my most basic needs, like nutrition, health, and medication.

My final challenge has been accepting that family and friends have set boundaries around my alcoholic words and behaviors. I am aware of my Jekyll and Hyde personality when actively drinking. My family's love comes now in the form of "tough love." I only know that if I have patience now, those I love and hold dear to my heart will come back to me, even if I arrive in heaven first.

LN

Finding God

I. IN THE WAFER

I was eleven years old when I became jealous over my best friend attending Catholicism classes. She was studying to be confirmed, and she went to class every Sunday—workbook on Jesus in hand and all. It's the first time I wondered, "why don't I go to church every Sunday?"

So, one Sunday, I was invited to church with her and her family. It came time to receive Communion and she convinced me that I was totally eligible to do so, being that my family was Irish Catholic and all. She filled me in on the rules; which hand gets placed over the other as I receive the wafer and such. The most important and stressed rule was that I let the wafer dissolve; under no circumstances should I chew. So, I accepted my wafer and as I headed back to my pew this sticky, putty-like substance began forming . . . I began choking on the wafer! I ended up having to leave the church service to get water, half choking to death, and I thought to myself: "Well, now I know there is a God because I just pissed him off!" It wasn't until years later that I realized she was just pranking me. It would have been perfectly acceptable to chew.

II. IN THE TREES

At fifteen years old, I came out about the abuse I suffered at the hands of my twisted step-father. He eventually pled guilty to his years of torment in court. I remember as I lay on my father's lap in that courtroom, sobbing my eyes out, I didn't quite understand why I was even there. And then, when his "punishment" was a fine and not a single day in jail, I thought, "maybe there is no God."

From there my journey spiraled a bit out of control. I ate magic mushrooms at eighteen and found "God" in the trees, in the grass, in the Earth. Then the spiral went downward, beyond the farthest recesses of my imagination of what darkness could be.

And now, here I sit today, having found the light. God is love. The love of my mother who has stood by my side. The love of strangers who see my own light. And two weeks from today, God will hopefully be with me in a courtroom once again . . . showing his love through mercy.

JILL

Dark Inky Night

The burden I face every day feels like walking through an inky black night. Each day feels dark and unclear. I feel as if I've gotten through some of the deep black night. I feel like I've gotten through some of the path, but not fully. I am still not seeing the light of day, just trying to find the right path and not stumble or hit into any trees . . . stay focused on what's ahead of me . . . that each step takes me closer to getting out of the dark, inky night.

CARA

Who I Am

I thought I was Money.
I thought I was Cocaine.
I thought I was the Streets.
I was Anger.
I was Rage.
I was Forgotten.
BUT—WHO AM I?

In the silence, who am I?
In the silence I find Self.
Behind this time is my heart.
In the silence, I hear my heart,
I hear my soul.

I was him, I was nothing.
My value was found in his dreams.
I was invisible, but I am not
who I thought I was. I thought
I was weak but today I realize
my strength and determination.
Today I know how it feels to truly love Self.
I understand unconditional love starts with Self.
Today I stand up for myself.
He cannot walk on me anymore.
He cannot have my sacredness,
he never deserved a piece of my heart;
but I gave him the whole thing
freely. My desire was so strong.
I needed him to want me,
so he had me; but never appreciated me.
He lost me, but I found me.
And I swear I'll never be
treated like that again.

Stacy

Permission to Breathe

Once I leave this place, will I have permission to breathe again? Will I have the strength to be strong and say no, to live a new life without my addictions? To start over again with a clean slate, to right the wrongs? Please, I beg you, I would like permission to breathe again. Without the grey clouds that are hanging over me; when the second chance is given and I prove to myself permission to breathe is granted.

MH

Invocation

I dedicate myself to healing, a thorough cleansing
   of my soul.
Exhausted by choosing misery. Now it's time
to shush the recording playing in my head.
How long can I rewind the same story?
Finding now that I can change the endings.
No longer allowing myself excuses to live in the
   wrong.
My heart is open to real forgiveness. My spirit
   starting to know
what it is like to fly free, without the weight of all
   my burdens.

BS

Longing to Be a Mother Again

. . . to be loved, needed
to be a mother again.
I just want my children to remember me,
say "that's My Mom"
know I still love and need them.

I want them to know they did nothing wrong by
    my not being around
for them to know I think of them always,
that they're still my precious angels and
I love them more than there are stars.

I want my life to be the way it was before I knew
    drugs
maybe then I would still have my children,
have contact with them, see them.

I want to be normal
to read them bed-time books again
to go back and be the one who taught them to ride
    a bike
be the one to send them to school
I want my babies to know that I am still here
and will never go anywhere
I want them to know how much I'm sorry.
I want to be able to just say "I love you" again
to be the mother they deserve
to hug and kiss them
play and laugh with them again.

I want my life back
to be a mother again . . .

DEBI

God Heard Me

I was only attempting to get in touch with my inner harmony, not to embark on a masterpiece. No walls came crashing down; the lights didn't flicker; and no angel appeared from some abyss that formed beneath my floating feet. Yet a simple old verse came into my head. It was a beautiful verse that was touching to me and let me know that God had heard my voice among the prevailing chatter. That he and I had a special moment. Because the distance and emptiness I've been feeling lately due to a wrench in my faith was gapped by him speaking to me with one of his many miraculous ways. Beauty that is constantly present.

MELISSA G

I Can!

Over the past few months, I've realized my life's patterns of not completing any task or goal I've set out to accomplish. I've always started head-first and enjoyed the pure excitement of being a part of and the start of any project, class, group I've committed to attend.

But over the years I've realized I've had many challenges, and the struggles were sometimes like huge mountainsides to climb; somewhere along the way I lost momentum. My fears, my shortcomings began to quietly ring out self-doubt. Questioning myself would become my second nature, and before long I'd believe I didn't belong or wasn't smart enough to figure it out and overcome the challenge, and I would end up quitting.

I've better yet come to know, Ladies, that over the last five years while I was kicking myself in the ass and making a mockery of myself each time I came up from that fetal position, I took something with me. I learned that I had a different way of seeing things, processing things, and how each project would over time be accomplished. I just had to interject with my self-loathing drug addiction and let that vice make me happy when I was feeling so low, like I couldn't complete anything because my self-doubt would suffocate me.

Although it's been a scary place for me to be, alone, feeling like I couldn't ask for help because of fear, I end up leaving feet first, never using my brain but letting the emotional foothold lead my way.

It's proven a very unhealthy pattern for me and each day I am learning to start one thing at a time and give it its space, honoring the time it needs to come alive, take action, and successfully complete what it is I've set out to accomplish.

It's a great feeling knowing I can no longer let fear drive me through this life of mine, and with each goal I check off my list, I am reclaiming my own worth and learning I CAN do anything, as long as I give it time and give it my all.

Tess

The Superpower I Want to Possess

The older I get, the more I wonder if I even want a superpower. Sure, they sound really cool.

Super-strength, *woo hoo!* I can pick up cars and chuck 'em. But who would I chuck 'em at?

Invisibility. Yes! I could walk around without being seen. But would I walk into places I shouldn't be?

Fire. Fire. Sweet. But would I burn arbitrary things in my anger?

Aqua lungs. I know, right? But believe me, I would find a way to use that wrong.

Every superpower I think of keeps me thinking, "with great power comes great responsibility."

So, I would probably be like Catwoman; when I'm good, I'm good, but when I'm bad, watch out! Not exactly a super hero, not exactly a super super villain. Just an average lady.

So as for superpowers, NO THANK YOU! I have enough to handle for now. I'm just gonna be like Batman and Robin. Neither have "superpowers." But they both have super wits and use the things around them to help others. 'Cause quite frankly, I don't want "great responsibility"—regular responsibility is hard enough.

BILLIE

Sick of Trouble

Have you ever felt like doing the same thing over and over again gets boring or maybe even sickening? Well, I can definitely say that I'm sick of being in trouble. Beating people up. Selling drugs. Using drugs. There comes a time when enough is enough. I am twenty-two years old and have been doing time since I was eighteen. Always looking over my shoulder, running from the cops, spending $200 a week on flush kits. Going back and doing sanction after sanction. Getting caught up with the wrong people.

Well, it's time for me to leave that all behind and start a real mature adult life. Being inside this disgusting, awful horrible place is not for me anymore. I have grown up and learned from my mistakes. I'm all done with the bad things. I'm gonna be good.

I get out in May and this time I'm staying out. No more hanging out with the wrong people. Get a real job and be a mom. If it's not positive, then I'm not doing it. I'm leaving all the negative behind.

TG

I Am a Turtle

I am a turtle, a hard shell I call my home,
full of what no one knows except me.

My hard back protects me so I can survive
through anything, any circumstances.
It protects my soft heart.

   I wonder—
   are young turtles mean? or do time
   and life make them hard and bitter?
   do they get angry when their shell dulls,
   elements have taken their toll?
   is it just the turtle alone there inside
   the darkness?

My shell appears hollow so I can pull myself inside
and wait. Retreating inward whenever I'm afraid.
Nobody can see me, just my shell.

I blend in, seem to go unnoticed.
I might even seem harmless. But nobody knows
what's in my shell. I choose who I want
within my shell. Once in, there's no getting out.

Life beats on my back,
but it does not break me.

Stacy

Like an Apple

I feel like an apple that was once growing from a beautiful, healthy tree. Then the tree swayed in the wind one day, and the apple fell to the ground. When the apple fell, it got bruised. Then a worm crawled inside of the apple as it rotted because it was no longer part of the beautiful tree. Before the apple fell, it had been turning different colors and was growing so well. Now that it has fallen, it will no longer be. This is how I relate to an apple because now I look back on how I was doing, and how quickly things change when you fall. But hey, there is still room to change, and become an apple pie that everybody loves. I can also relate to being an apple on a tree, and somebody picks you instead of all the others to be the victim.

JOELLEN

To Be a Strawberry

My life needs much tending and nurturing care, for my life can be as fragile, fragrant and delicious as the vine-ripened strawberry, standing brightly on the vine awaiting someone's desire to taste it; and once plucked to feel the plumpness and smell the sweet aroma, your mouth watering to take a taste. You taste the strawberry as though it were a forbidden delight, the juice running down your chin. You smile to yourself while imagining all sorts of scenarios possible for those strawberries—shortcake, cheesecake, whipped cream, dipped in chocolate, on a cake, or simply the way they are. My life is that strawberry with endless possibilities, just waiting to be plucked.

NORAJEAN

My Many Layers

Like an onion, my life has many layers. The innermost layers, tender and green, like my infancy and childhood, not completely even all the way around as I am just learning about things then. The next layer, innocent but getting larger, so filled with juice and thick, the "meat" of the onion. The further layers getting thinner as the years seem to fly by until I am a wife, no longer just someone's child. And then I became a mother as well, and now my children have grown and don't physically need me anymore, and the layer is even thinner, and eventually my skin will wrinkle and age like an onion, skin brown and fragile to the touch, until I too am buried under the ground like the onion root that grows new life to the next generation of onion.

MICHELE

Nine Months to Adulthood

In nine months my adult self would be here because I would be a mom, and I knew I had to change not just for myself, but for my child. How could I be a child having a child? So I knew it was time to grow . . . grow into the adult I had to be, the adult I was bound to be, the adult who knew how to take care of a child.

I knew in nine months I would no longer be able to go out and play whenever I wanted to. I knew I would have no more playtime of my own, no more running free like I did as a child because in nine months I would have a child who would need a mom. In nine months my adult self would be here.

CZ

Yin and Yang

My eyes sparked, representing life, reaching out to cast upon beauty, anything that compliments my eyes' beauty, wanting only to see goodness. Advantages within my grasp, life that's fulfilling, wholesome, of purity.

My eyes darkened, black rims dull my beautiful blue eyes to dark shades of gray, sunken in where no light comes from, I'm reaching out for death, cold, clammy figures, glass tunnels, my addiction. Cloudy smoke rolls away from me as I slump back and refuse to look away from what frightens me.

Life and death are my symbols of yin and yang. My addiction and sobriety hold the balance to this transforming life of mine. Stepping out of the darkness into the light gives me fresh air, leaving the black smoke and destruction behind. Hoping my addiction won't creep up on me again, doing it to me another time.

TESS

Out of the Box

Life out of the box—do I dare lift the top and peer out? What will I find out beyond the boundaries and limitations I have set for myself—my safe haven, the familiarity of my limits comforting in an indescribable way? Should I venture out? How far can I go? Always hearing the words echo in my mind, "You can be whatever you want to be, do whatever you want to do, go wherever you want to go!"

But these things take courage, drive and determination. Do I have what it takes? If I were to listen to the voices that haunt me, I would have to say, "I think not!" But it's my voice wanting to shout above the din of those haunting words, "Hear me—I am more than what you say. I can and I will step outside, because I can now. The limits once set to keep me within lie like broken twigs on the ground. I have found my courage, my determination, my strengths and my voice; and I will not be stilled any longer."

Living outside the box will be a new and exciting adventure, a journey into the vast unknown, one I am looking forward to, beginning my life anew. The marquee is flashing, "COMING SOON."

NORAJEAN

Afraid to Leave

I'm not afraid to stay.
I'm afraid to leave.
To put my life in his hands.
I'm afraid to give him the control.
Does he really know what's best for me?
I'm not afraid to put myself in a position of possible failure; but I am afraid to place myself on a path to success.
Fear runs deep in my heart. No matter what way I turn, I'm not meeting someone's standards.
I know my life is gonna be hard, but I'm confident that I can do this. That I'll be OK.
I just wanna go home.
I'm tired of time.
I'm afraid to be on my own in a place I don't know. With people I don't know.
My pride gets in the way. I'm afraid to ask for help. I'm afraid to be rejected. At least at home I know the area; I'm more comfortable. If I need something I can ask for it. Without shame. And without fear.
I'm afraid I'll never get to spend time with my nephew. Or my mother.
I'll be caught up in my own life; then it will be too late.
I'll live a life of regret because time is precious.
I can't get back these years; and I can't give them back the time I took.
The foundation of me was weak. But now is strong.
The cost now outweighs the benefit.
How hard are you willing to struggle?
It can never be worse than it already has been.

STACY

Closing the Door to Chaos

Hundreds of miles from my home is where I woke up this morning. Haunted at night by demons in my dreams. Lost in darkness during the day. Wondering when this all began and where I was when I opened the door to chaos.

My mind and soul shut closed like a home in winter. Wandering the same drab hallways day in, day out. I was numb for so many moonrises and sunsets that I don't remember what a sunrise looks like anymore. I just went through the motions for many days, weeks now.

Something has happened, yet again, without my knowledge. A door slammed shut, not the door that keeps me locked in this cement building. It is the door to chaos. There goes another door, and another. Darkness. Frustration. Sorrow. They all slam, hopefully for good this time. I think for a moment and question what's really going on.

Then I see it; it's the sun rising. I realize I'm hundreds of miles from home. No one can access me here. I can call only those who see the sun rising the same as I do. I now have the strength to close and lock the doors of my past and darkness.

RAVEN

Choosing Life

I choose life over drugs any day. Drugs screwed up my life. And took my children away. I hate drugs. They used to be my best friend—I didn't think I could live a day without them.

Drugs are an awful part of life. And I feel sorry for anyone who is or has ever had to deal with that in their lives. I know, 'cause it owned me for sixteen years of mine. I've only been clean and sober for five months and ten days, and I feel the best I've felt in my entire life.

I love my life today. Not chasing a high all day; not trying to get a fix. My life made me and everyone that actually cared about me sick. Some didn't want to talk to me. See me. Some were scared they'd get a phone call that I'd been found dead. That scares me now about other people. It just happened to my cousin.

I'm not perfect. But I'm glad that's not me anymore!

CS

Hope

Hope never died while I took my steps toward wrong. In fact, every time my choice was finalized, hope for one reason or another tied the commitment together. We always found hope to heal me from any circumstance that otherwise distracted me from pain or discomfort. Hope gave me the opportunity to freely choose. Not only does it give me the sense of freedom; but the power to pray. Sitting just where I want and meditate, speak to my God, lighting my truth, and casting aside doubt. Hope is everlasting, it never really dies within our world. It's passed along from you to me and spread infectiously to another. Hope is what has saved me and encouraged me along to fight, become; and its strength is in numbers alone.

TESS

Words

The best life lessons are learned in the midst of the overwhelming, and best understood after the storm has cleared. I wish someone had told me—

that my words hold more power than my body; that love is an action and touch is only a channel to express the choice to love. I wish someone had told me—

how I feel usually only lasts for a moment; and how I act leaves an impact not only on myself but on those around me. I wish someone had told me—

that you can't take back words no matter how hard or long you try. That it is my words and not the "sticks and stones."

LM

Closet of Secrets

We head into my closet, where a lot of my secrets are held. I keep trying on all my old stuff. When will I learn to just throw out what doesn't fit? But I still keep it, push it just a little further down the rod. I have to remember to save room in my closet, because I know there's a lot more to fit inside. Maybe one day I'll be able to at least bury some in the way back of my closet.

Melissa G

Learning to Let Go

All of my feelings that I have kept inside—about all the bad things that I have done—are finally coming out. I am learning to deal with them. I now have the courage to talk about these things. Before when I was out and getting high, I kept all these feelings bottled up, not wanting to feel them, not caring about them or how they affected the people I loved. Now some of these people have passed on or have moved on. Can I blame myself? Yes, for not treating them how I would if I was sober. Can I change the past? No. But I have let courage take over; I now talk about these things. Can I change my future? Yes. Have I? I am learning; learning to let go.

BIG D

"Hold nothing back, learn to find ease in risk"[2]

How is this possible? Doesn't the word "risk" itself evoke feelings of danger, insecurity, and fear? It's risky to dive off a cliff into water below. How do I know I won't be crushed by rocks unseen beneath the surface of blue?

Holding nothing back is still, however, my greatest desire for this year. I want to live in this skin, this beautifully tangled mess of eccentricity, imperfection, and emotion. I want to let my light shine. I can feel the glow growing, warmth, humor; a spectacular array of characteristics that have made me the person I am today.

I want to risk things larger than a cliff-dive into the ocean: living my dreams, allowing myself to accept that I am a writer, growth without a man to fall back on (or to have to hold up, which has generally been my life's scenario). I want to be at ease with the fact that I love myself, and don't need or care about the way others perceive me.

I want to be courageous and prove the doubters wrong. I have been burning for far too long; I have scars so deep they reach my soul. With all that burning, there must be a light of some kind and I see it . . . through my sober eyes, through my laughter, through the reflections of loved ones beginning to see possibility in me once again.

So, how is this possible? I may not have all the answers yet; but ask me again next year, because that is exactly what I intend to do . . . release, unclench, believe that anything is possible. This is my new beginning.

Jill

⁓

---

[2] John O'Donohue, "For a New Beinning, *To Bless the Space Between Us: A Book of Blessings* (New York: Doubleday, 2008), 14.

A Solid Place for My Feet

A sound place for my feet is a happy heartbeat
no hard place to fall, the stance is flat, enemies all
    fade to black.
I do recall feeling that safe harbor
where the moonlit trees sprinkle waves of glamour.
And up above, a shooting star, sparkles bright, even
    from afar.
The steady rock to me appears at the peak of a
    mountain
where I've conquered my fears. Down below at the
    water's edge,
the pillars break for sweet revenge.
I would like to climb up even higher,
I'll just close my eyes and walk a thin wire.
Because at the end of the rocky dirt road
I'll find a new place that I can call home;
now all those memories deplete
I've now got a solid place for my feet.

MELISSA G

Arrive and Celebrate

What an invitation to life,
a promise for a brighter future
to have, to hold.
Someone special to spend life with,
commit to a journey neither knows,
willing us deeply into a kinder world.

I think of this rebirth as a blessing
that God has gently placed before me,
guiding my soul to his wondrous land,
where it's less complicated
and where love is the center pulling at you,
giving substance to my new life.

Leaving behind a lot of pain that's
been sifted through and processed,
taking with me the lessons it had to offer.
Not swaying to the memories or beliefs
that keep me imprisoned.

Freedom, hope and a new way to express myself
among comforting men and women.
Learning there is more to life than my past.
Believing in the process to overcome
life's sometimes bitter challenges
and life's many disruptions.
Knowing my freedom of choice is still mine,
but having an adult mind
that's capable and sound and thriving.

Arriving and celebrating my new ways,
my new family and the many precious hands
that will guide me along my path.

TESS

Do I Dare?

You took away my childhood,
my trust, my love, my heart.
You took away my innocence
by tearing me apart.

You took away so many years,
you caused me so much pain.
And these things you did to me
were only for your gain.

Now the choice is mine to make:
the things from me you longed
to take, I'll get them back,
you'll see, you'll see.

You'll never be
the death of me.
I'll rise, I'll rise.

I'm almost there.
The question is:
"Do I dare?"

SARAH

"Welcoming home all who in hope knock"[3]

A yearning started, a spark of hope. The first murmur of the universe taking shape in your mind. Your search for self, for meaning. formulation of being. A biography in the making. Where shall the wind take you today? What omen will you see to push you toward your destiny? What will you see when you look ahead, behind? what greatness can you perceive? The years pass, still pressing toward your treasure, your destiny. The great brass ring. Do you see it? Is it still there? Don't miss out. Don't give up on your treasure. Keep searching. There's always a glimmer. In your golden years, there is gold even when the mirror sees gray. Know you have taken every chance, every step, finding your way in the world in your own way. Welcome home, all who in hope knock!

LUCINDA

ᔆ

---

[3] Rev. Peter Skaller, "Advent Poem—Hope" (December 11, 2011), published on thechristiancommunity.org website.

Blind to the Future

She is so young, so naive, so innocent.
Behind those honey-colored eyes is a young woman, lost.
She is searching for something that will take her years to find.
How I pity her. She does not see the treacherous path in front of her.
I pound my fist up against the thick window. I scream her name.
She can't hear or see me. I am beyond her reach.
She is swimming and gasping in a world created by her own false truth.
Appearing confident and carefree, but she is removed and cold on the inside.
She is more afraid than anyone I know.
I whisper to myself, *"Please don't be afraid. You are stronger and more courageous than you know."*
She doesn't acknowledge my pleas.
I weep for her because of the pain she will endure.
All the while smiling because I know that she will endure.
One day the storms inside will quiet, and she will find peace she never knew before.
I press my hand up against the smooth glass.
She looks my way and smiles, wistfully. Does she see me yet?
I long to hold her and comfort her.
But this is a journey she must take alone. So I back away.
She must do this in order to become the happy and confident woman I am today.

RAVEN

What I Would Say to a Poem

What I would say to a poem is how
my life has twisted and turned, never
remaining stable for very long. How
my own inner demons transcended
to my very soul, to live there and fester
until my life began to rot. Of how
I longed for things, things that always seemed
just out of my reach—happiness, love, peace
and contentment. Of how I resented those
around me that had achieved those very things.

Of how my dreams fell one by one
off the side of my reality, drifting away
as if in space, with my heart longing
to reach out and bring them back. But
I could not grasp them. I would tell of how
one day, when my life felt the most lost, I
reached out and asked God to save me,
to give me back my hopes and dreams,
to allow me to feel happiness, love, peace
and contentment. And much to my amazement—
He DID!

NORAJEAN

Follow the River

Today can start a new beginning,
a new way to live worth living.
It's time to speak the truth about my addictions,
so many I have that cause me friction.
I want to be more honest on how bad they really
    are;
afraid that when I do, it will leave one more per-
    manent scar.
Know deep down the truth that will set me free;
and my addiction won't become my destiny.
If I let it all out and become who I want to be—
'cause I know this person and life are just not me.
I say my eyes are open wide
when really all I do is hide.
But if and when I really give it a try,
I know that's when I can truly hold my head up
    high.
My chance is here, right now, to let it all go
right down the river and let that good part of me
    show.
I do feel as if God has a path for us, too;
both parts of me as I do!

CRYSTIE

Running Free

I keep on running through it all
spinning round and round trying not to fall,
jumping through hoops, running wild and free
trying to figure out who I want to be.
Do I want to be known for my past,
or do I crave that life that'll last?
Tired of the not knowing
wondering if it's really showing
how lost and scared I am of this disease.
If people really knew, I'd just freeze
in fear of what others may think when I say, "no,"
wishing I could just let this all go
'cause I'm tired of living a lie.
It's time to stop caring and give it a try!

Billie

Getting Out

I feel like crying just to let out what's inside.
Spineless emotions my addiction tries to hide,
a distant memory my face cannot deny.
In pain filled, my honesty
is the only way to let it out. I've tried
all my life my own way.

Now it's on to longer days
of doing it "their way." I've lain in my bed for days,
calm as can be while people around me
try to provoke me. Their hidden pain turned to laughter
spooks me only because I know what it is they are after.

I push ahead knowing what's to come—
a big house filled with women
a new journey, recovery to name the important one.
I dig deep inside and bring forth what's really necessary
to travel: light, because I'm fighting for my life.
It's about to be a long and scary fight.

TESS

Starting Anew

I. SPRING CLEANING

Spring cleaning is kind of what I am doing here, in prison, to myself. Getting rid of the old unlawful me to start anew. Cleaning out the guilty feelings for past mistakes. Following the law to continue my life with Joe and my parents. Giving my children, who are old enough to take care of themselves, the freedom to do so. Starting a new career now that my old one is going to be unavailable to me because of my crime. Freed from parenting 24/7 and starting my life of helping my mother cope with premature memory loss caused by age. Starting our lives over when we get out, with no guilt or wrongdoing so we can be new people. God speeding us on our way down the righteous path . . .

II. CARING FOR ME

Trying to take care of ME for the first time in a long time. I almost don't know how. Since my baby sister was born when I was 23 months old, I have always had someone to nurture and protect; and the Usual Suspects, the ones I usually take care of, are on the outside and beyond my reach. I can only take care of myself and those here who will let me help them. I find the need to take care of something to be overwhelming at times. I think I will actually have to learn how to put myself first. It is not something I was ever taught to do, nor was it ever encouraged. My roommate has tried to help me a bit, but it will be a long road. I like helping; and being able to help others brings me joy as much as it drains me.

Michele

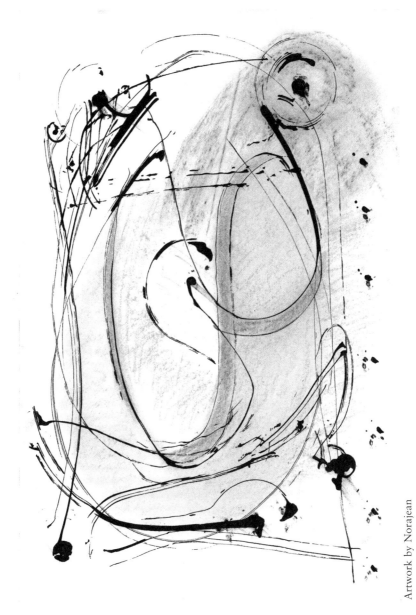

Artwork by Norajean

I Am Here

"God is an ocean of mercy . . . Collapse into God's arms and you'll weep like a child."

—RUMI

It is me, your daughter.
I am here, in your light.
Your grace has given me many blessings.
It is me whom you loved,
no matter the number of my faults.

I am here, broken before you,
ready to receive your glory.
I have taken many paths in this life,
which have taught me not to fear you;
for you gave me breath,
you gave me life,
and through these many circumstances,
you let me live.
I am of love and have been forgiven.

Please, show me what it is
you want from me.
I am at your mercy;
I am on bended knee
asking for you to hold me,
comfort me, show me
how to control my fear of the world.

Give me the strength, the power
to rise from the bondage of my addiction.
Clear my path of suffering
and give me your love.
I am right here,
ready to receive it,
live in it, breathe it,
and give it back to the world.

Please, release me;
I want to love you back,
the way you've always loved and cherished me.
I want to live my life as though
I am wrapped tightly in your arms,
not stranded out at sea
with no means to a life,
lost, forgotten, unforgiven, broken,
and with no direction to save me.

When I am strong enough,
when the time is right—
give me rest, clear my mind,
cleanse my soul, give me peace.
Let the flood of my emotions release,
renewing my passage into this life.
Rebuild my self-confidence.
Give me new life,
new encounters that enrich my life.
Encourage the energy that surrounds me
to be of peace and comfort.
I trust you,
you have never forsaken me.
Growth is key in my addiction.

TESS

Walk Me through the Door

"My grief imprisons me. Look! The key is here!"

—RUMI

It is here the lessons of introspection
have guided me with a new set of lenses
Years of savoring each tear, weeping away time,
letting go of this perception, and claiming my life
. . . closure of what was with all its strife

Unlocking my soul into a journey of more
Beauty awakens again—as I breathe in
Breaking out, the world opens her arms again
I have so much gratitude for what's in store

The feelings of impending doom no longer gloom
My internal shame chamber shuts the doors
I free myself from the guilt on the inside
Befriending this woman, I have become divine

Each tape that replays, I pause it and say,
you are not that scared little girl, but a woman
    today
Defending my values, integrity, eccentricity
with obscurity to settle the score

Observing lessons to take on my own,
the past no longer defines me
The present here, teaching lessons
to take into my future and honor my core

My love for this life
has new meaning with this release
I am not made for this journey,
yet glad God has walked me through this door

TONYA

Wellspring of Hope

Hope is the light post that points you toward destiny. Struggle is the road-sign reminding you of your accomplishments along the way.

Lucinda

∞

The Light of Life[4]

"Leaving behind nights of terror and fear"
I say goodbye to you, my dear.
It will be a long hard road, I'm sure;
as long as I keep going, my mind should stay pure.
I'm sorry our relationship has come to an end
as well as all the bad energy you send.
Our relationship one-sided, you controlled it all
and every step I took, all I did is fall.

"I rise into a daybreak that's wondrously clear."
With that empowering moment, I have no fear.
I won't let your trickery drag me down anymore.
Now I'm the one that has tricks in store.
Just like the rest of life, darkness is broken with
    shining light
and I will always continue the everlasting fight.
If in life you get back up every time you fall
you know with certainty that you can have it all.

JD

∞

---

[4] Based on lines from Maya Angelou, "Still I Rise," in *And Still I Rise: A Book of Poems by Maya Angelou* (New York: Random House, 1978), 41.

Seed of Faith

Faith is like a seed planted, an idea first taking root nestled down deep, protected. The root begins to branch out seeking nourishment. The shell around the seed breaks open and we see the furled stalk curled up tight. As time passes, the stem slowly begins its journey to the top, to freedom. Once it breaks through, it begins to unfurl, become straight. We begin to see the bud of the leaves and flower, closed tightly for a time, until they begin to trust and open to the world.

A little at first, then more and more until faith has become the beauty of the rose.

NORAJEAN

Prayer at the Crossroads

I have come to the crossroads
of my life on this journey
I have been traveling,
several times prior believing
each time: this is the last.
Curious, as to why I am coming
to this place again—
Are my indiscretions so large?
Is my heart eternally cold?
I pray to the Lord for forgiveness.
My Savior, take away my sins.
May I never see this razor wire again.
May I come to a place where my spirit is free.
I am lost within my soul,
and I can't break free.

TONYA

Serving Sentences

I am coming to realize that all my decisions affect my family, especially my children and their own lives individually. I made choices knowing that the end results could send me to jail. Feeling like I would be the only one serving the time, when in reality my children are also serving my sentence from the outside.

Big D

On Vulnerability

If you have all you could ever ask for, want, or need, what then do you hope for? You most certainly wouldn't want for a strenuous voyage. Only when you've caught wind of the sacred treasure that you're missing out on does your journey begin. As you set out in search of the missing piece, the struggle is laying out your very first step.

Melissa G

Middleman No Longer

Growing up, I was placed in between my parents
during their arguments.
As a teen till my twenties, I played the role of a
supervisor,
there always in between our employees and my
father, the boss.
From my twenties till now at thirty-one, I played
the middleman
in my addiction to drugs.
I also played the ball boy in my marriage today,
and my parents,
my kids, and their father.
I draw for other inmates for their families.
Well now I suppose I deserve a shot of empowering
that middleman.
I will not get in your fights.
I will be the boss.
I will not buy or do drugs.
I will not get in anyone's fights.
I will not go over your father's head.
I will keep drawing pictures to make people happy.
The only middleman of my life was to make others
happy,
but now I'll only do it on my watch.
'Cause I'm not a lil' girl, or a teen, or even an addict
you can push around any more.

FLIP

Choosing Happiness

I spoke with you briefly on the phone today. It's been a while, hasn't it? The voice is familiar but something is off with you. I struggle to grasp tightly to the new, different you who is willing his essence through the distance on the phone connection between us.

I married into this life; I didn't consciously choose it. Or did I? Am I an adrenaline junkie, a dopamine addict looking for the next most pleasurable solution in pill, powder or smoke-able substance? Did I consciously choose this life, or did I simply, passively allow it to happen?

You say the next, greatest hit is with a needle; that I'll love it and I'll feel amazing . . . Really? Will I? Or will I only feel guilt when I examine what I've become?

I want to grow and change with you; I want our new beginning this year. But I'm scared. I thought we'd grow in a new direction but not this particular one. The scary part is that if I face my own truth, my heart wants to take flight and jump into these murky waters fully submerged with you. To go to the unknown and back with you. But what I want and what I'll do are two separate ideas. What I want and what I *need* is too varied.

So, is the beginning that has been quietly forming, unnoticed by you, about to sprout wings and fly out my mouth with fury? Or am I still unable to leave what I must outgrow? When people ask me what I want in life, I only have one answer: "to be happy." Will your way make me happy? The seduction of the needle, whom I've never had the pleasure of meeting personally, began years ago when I'd hear legends of his feats. His simple intense glory, with the thrust of the plunger into the syringe and the sharp metal tip puncturing beings with euphoria. He'd go again and again until there was no more pleasure.

So then, what was next? Only pain? Was it worth it? And why do I seek the answer?

TIFFANY H

Yearning to Be Seen

Your perception of me needs to shift, if ever so
  slight.
I must tell you, your view of me was definitely
  skewed.
However, that might possibly be my fault.
I hid who I am from you, and tucked it out of sight.
I did not trust myself or anyone else enough to let
  them see in.
Many apologies for my countless mistakes.
But, I will ONLY apologize just once, because we
  must move on.
I may have seemed flighty or foolish; but I am
  clever and calculating, always thinking, observ-
  ing, analytical and maybe a little forgetful.
I seemed like I had many secrets and not the most
  honest.
Truth be told, I was! The secrets have been revealed
  and honestly? Well, I am ready to tell and hear
  it all.
You probably didn't like me too much.
I was chatty (about nothing) and tried way too
  hard.
I still enjoy talking (to those who listen) and I will
  not waste my breath on any other lost cause.
I can be jealous, envious and yearned for what I
  didn't have. I coveted "things" far too much.
I still want, still yearn, but it is different now.
I yearn for you to now know the "real" me!
I yearn for you to see who I truly am and help me
  show the entire world.
I yearn to be happy and peaceful.
I yearn for you to trust and respect me.
I desperately need you to love me.
"Do you see what I see?" I begged at the reflection
  staring back at me.

RAVEN

Things I'd Rather You Not Know

It's how it happened that's shameful. The thought of you finding out makes me want to run and hide. I feel selfish, too, knowing you are my father, the one who watched me grow; and how would you have known, it was hidden so well. My own pain is just too much to try to even begin to feel; but watching your whole world crumble makes this much more confusing.

I don't want you to remember this, but we have really no choice. The things I didn't want you to know came out. My only thoughts are: can you still love me the same; and are you still going to be here to support me? I'm scared to death to be alone a minute longer with all the hurt and shamefulness that's been going on inside. A void within me that has shattered my perception of who I am and what it is I should be.

I've learned over time how to push the pain and fear deeper down, just for the sake of my own well-being. On the outside, I'm looking like the woman who's reached her beauty; but inside is the killer. I'm all these mixed emotions, bottled up tightly, trying to figure out if I let out the true thing I feel within me, will you love me, accept me, and fill me with your pride? Somewhere along the way, I got lost in others' plans; but today, with your help, I can better begin to figure out how to feel like a woman of self-worth and confidence.

TESS

Inside the Closet

She is playing in a room
stuffed dolls on the bed
alone, quiet, content
the sound of the back door
creaking open, slamming shut,
the hairs on her neck stand
with soldiers' attention.
She quickly slides the wooden
closet doors open and slips inside,
pushes her mother's dresses and
makes a spot in the back
then carefully, ever so quietly,
she slides the doors shut
darkness, utter darkness
deafening silence, like out of
the tell-tale heart, her breath
and the pounding inside her
eardrums are what keep her company
he will never find her here
and in that closet she is left—alone.

A teenager laughs, blows smoke
rings, plays teenage games
pushing invisible boundaries
she falls in love, she is a wreck
she gets her heart broken
she falls apart, she grows older.

A young woman ice skates on quicksand
with each stroke of her bladed foot
she moves forward and downward
together in an exquisitely spirited motion
she dances, she moves
she grabs a partner, loses him
in the dance, grabs another
suddenly she is stuck, petrified
she looks around
swallowing the sand
surrounded in darkness, alone
she struggles and falls farther still.

A slightly older woman emerges
finger to her lips, a hush
hands reaching through the darkness
she pulls through and is returned
to a closet
with a wooden door
slides it open
smiles, sighs, laughs, sobs
she pulls back the dresses
and reaches for the girl.

JILL

We Have a Plan

When I'm mad or in pain, I say He doesn't hear
    my prayers;
then, when it's obvious He does I'll proclaim, *He
    does! I'm aware!*
For years I said song was how I felt He was there;
but when out of church a different life I had, I
    didn't really care.
Last week I felt an old way of life and I opened my
    heart and let God back in my life.
I still have struggles. I still have pain. But when I
    scream and yell,
it doesn't feel the same; and I want others to know
    it's not just a game.
I think in my head, still, *why is it again happening
    to me?*
Didn't I ask God to take care of me?
Then I remember the good and then pray like I
    should;
I ask Him to carry me and He lets me rest, it's less
    scary for me.
I know I'll fall, but I'll get up again, 'cause I know
    I love God and He's more than a friend.
It might take time or the rest of my life to show all
when they speak of their memories and I hope they
    aren't small.
Where life takes me I must go, and it tires me so;
but it's what I go through, maybe how He speaks
    to you!
So remember, all of you, who see me be dumb—that
    in my heart I'll always succumb.
I'll cry out, *OH GOD PLEASE HELP* and it may
    seem to only be a yelp.
But really, I'm praying; even if you don't think I
    know what I'm saying.
It may seem small, but I'm giving it up, is all.

ANGIE

In the Wounded Bird Sanctuary

Like a sweet yellow songbird, I just wanted to be free. Free from the torment, yelling, making up. Staying happy but wondering when my song would be taken away again. You were my dove, the two of us sat side by side on the telephone wire. It was dangerous, full of life, but we stayed together. I wonder why. Where, oh where was that damn cat when I needed help? I guess he got me now. Here I am in the wounded bird sanctuary, have not died of a broken heart yet. But my wings feel clipped. Will it always feel like this—little pokes to my fragile body that remind me of us? Or will I heal? Oh, so bad do I want to heal! To fly singing my song, my happy praise to the world, to the sad people hoping to make someone's day. And to God, who restored my song. Well, this is what I want. I'm scared about doing this whole thing over, but I am not all gone. I have plenty of life left in me. But I won't let my self always live like that again!

CARA

Swapping State for Federal

Sifting through the papers, the cards, the letters received; all the things I held in my cell as important, things that helped me survive the past year.

And now I watch my hands drop armfuls of memories into the recycling bin as I prepare to move on. I will gift away the necessities, clothing and hygiene; whatever small tokens I have collected that may make another woman's stay a bit more comfortable.

I will mail out a selection of cards, pictures, names and addresses of those who've touched my life and whom I cherish enough to keep in contact.

And soon one morning the call will come, where I will have minutes to say goodbye to the place that has forever changed me.

With only the clothes on my back, and my head held high expressing the bravest face I can muster, I will prepare to walk down the halls that have held me in, held me down, and also held me up. A year and a lifetime, an unscripted ballet.

I will walk into booking, receive my shackles and cuffs, and I will be prepared for wherever the Feds take me. Because each prison is a building with different colored walls, different guards; each cell is a place to lay my head.

I am prepared for the unknown as much as I can be because I have found freedom in faith that this is only the beginning and not the end.

JILL

Goodbye

Please, let me loose to wander leeward.
Let me roam this way and that.
I, no longer, am a prisoner to you.
I refuse to be chained to you any longer.
We have been bound to one another
for far too long.
Why are you so afraid to let me go?
There is always someone else to take my place.
I have grown weary of the games
we play every day.
This used to be fun, now it's boring.
Honestly, we are a pathetic duo.
We are caught in the same cycle.
I am no longer believing your lies!
Who do you think you are any way?
You are no longer master and I, slave.
I will take a stand and break free.
There is no way we can remain friends.
Sorry, it's time for me to go.
We will not meet ever again.
You are no longer my destiny.
You are merely a glimpse of my past.

RAVEN

Collective Insight

Writings in this section reflect the truly communal focus of the entire writinginsideVT program. Each week, after hearing one another's words shared aloud, listeners "read back" to one another phrases that resonated with them during the readings. These phrases are then woven together in the week between meetings to create "found poems," raising all the voices in one collective piece. These are among the most cherished aspects of our weekly circles as women vie to read this work aloud, tickled to identify their own and each others' lines as the poem unfolds. Each "found poem" is also packed with poignancy and insight. While each poem encapsulates a particular theme, together they speak to a shared experience of growth and insight.

Artwork by Norajean

Sacred Heart

The story in my heart is of my Creator who, in the beginning, created the earth, the sun, the sky, and all. He saw that it was good.

Life went on for a time. Things began to go wrong with humanity. So He sent his only begotten Son to show us the way, the truth, and the life. His heart and His life he gave for us all.

This is His sacred heart.

NORAJEAN

A Journey Started, a Spark of Hope

I wasn't arrested, I was rescued
in a lot of old fashioned ways.
fifteen months on the inside
demanded small but important repairs:
open heart, changing my ways
to control what I think and feel;
to be myself in my entirety—
wisdom walker, fire woman.

After losing so much it is important to step back,
pointing to the one and only hope to keep you
moving on. Most of us could never imagine
that hope hadn't died, buried in pain.
Each tear contains a little spark of aliveness,
real possibility for a biography in the making
dissipating the inky black light.

Your search for self grows better with attention,
magically produces more love no matter what,
reflected every day in what greatness you
can perceive. There is always a glimmer of gold
even when the mirror sees gray.
It has come true for me.

Turn the corner of loneliness carrying hope within;
watch the lights twinkle as you pray,
starting your life over again. Keep searching.
Knowing you have taken every chance
will always be your hope.

Haunted by Demons

Is it something I may dream about tonight,
clearing out the reactionary cesspool
of emotional bondage?
Environments where I don't belong
come along like a twister—
I stray away, battered and bruised,
caught momentarily unaware.
Shock of unexpected thunder
traps me in that ever-tightening vice
holding in the sadness, the madness, the hate.
Lost so long in running and hiding,
I am haunted at night by demons
choking off new tender shoots.
I don't remember sunrise anymore,
always looking over my shoulder
and sick of being in trouble.

Do I have strength to close and lock the doors
leaving all the negative behind
these same drab hallways?

Tough Transition

A caged animal
eyes staring wildly
frozen in time,
in pain from the past—

It might as well be me.
I don't know who I am—
I lost me.
Why can't I move forward?

Gross and disgusting
in your eyes,
my heart sank.
I cleaned for hours,
numbing myself,
my mind enveloping my sanity.

The sky turns black,
lightning snaps,
leering faces peek from
commotion in the background,
cursing; fear and confusion
still alive,
deep-ridden—
I can't quite move,
let go of my fear.

I hold onto hope—
small beam of light—
seek serenity
ready to climb
true to who I am.

The dawning light will free me
from leg-irons and eyeliner
for what God has created me to be.
If we don't guard each others' souls, who will?

Always Wanting

I've battled with my own fear
to give you whatever you wish—
your heart or your mother's dream for you,
need for open space unfilled.

The bucket of my open mouth
is all I've ever wanted—
love and acceptance abundant,
stories and laughter,
your smile from ear to ear.

Through miles and miles of cold
you lit small worlds into being.
I heard that voice years ago,
every minute of me and you
until my demon pushed everyone away.

Then things got really tricky—
unknown, unplanned.
I peel myself off the ground
hungry for myself, hungry for you.

෮

I Have Been Known

I have been known as
self-righteous protector, for
ugly violence in public, to
wrap words around my listener,
not think it through, say
hateful words, cause
pain and heartache; to pull
myself up, share what I have, listen
past my ability to comprehend; be afraid
of not being accepted, right; angry,
a pain in the ass, alone and unknown,
cold, homeless, dirty, hungry; known
to do anything wild and crazy, yet
never been known to know me.

I've never been known
to have hopes and dreams,
be still, feel the warmth;
I just wanted to be seen,
so grateful for the smallest of things.

I so often doubt myself, a child
who depends on reassurance
tired of proving myself as worthy;
the crouching tiger
a sponge to absorb
a seed planted, an idea
a journey to freedom.

My body is scared but my heart soars
choosing courage over fear
(something I don't have).
One day it will find me. I just know.
I have faith in time. If your heart is good
you stand a good chance until faith
has become the beauty of the rose.

Empty Vessel

My mind is an empty vessel
not wanting to remember where I've been;
my foolish pride,

empty spaces left by time and poor decisions
longing for words, something to do
to fill the void; alone, afraid

generally lacking confidence,
my heart feels so hurt.
I wish I could become a sponge,

sift, sort, store ideas for tomorrow
be filled with every gift—
seasons that cycle,

vessel of hope and joy.
I want my full heart back,
the heart God gave me.

Emptiness and Fullness

I lost everything, including myself;
longed for something to make me feel whole.
Life's lessons rammed down my throat,
I learned to love myself by being betrayed.

Broken and damaged being
curved into elegant skin,
longing changed at a moment's notice
into a peaceful model that seemed to glide, not step.

When I was young I fell a lot,
hit rock bottom struggling to find happiness,
slender shoulders that screamed femininity;
the hurts I have caused others
an aching hole not human.

I could never seem to find all at once
all I am meant to be. I long for spiritual strength
to let go this melodramatic place, a lifelong struggle
to change. I forgive myself, have fallen
in love with myself—wouldn't trade it for anything.

Inside Looking Out

Imagine time in slow motion—
our seasons have slumbered on,
filled up the silence between us;
stored images for my heart camera
slowly, reluctantly giving way
to reach those few hours of sunlight,
the moon that guides us through
the long distance howl.

We begin all over again.
Listen for sound, watch what's around you;
each day has a new smell.
Red can mean so many languages
of feeling within the self.
When not successful we all feel the same way—
the foreign language of truth. At its best and worst
we separate, we fall apart, don't even speak
the same language, our differences so clear. Yet
you are powerful—I am powerful.

Dedication

Exhausted by choosing misery,
allowing excuses to live in the wrong,
rewinding the same story
dizzying myself with chaos—
I don't know how to stop.
This time away has been incredibly tough,
this week a true test of faith.

Normally, I would say the stain of bitterness
is a way for others to validate me, see me.
But we are given what we need.

And so I dedicate myself to tranquility of spirit,
health, well-being and personal healing;
to the work of my sobriety,
praying for a second chance.

I dedicate myself to humility and grace
wisdom and poise; to fight for the silent,
be their voice resilient and unique.

I dedicate myself to the little girl inside of me
who needs to laugh, play, roll on the ground.

I dedicate myself to the daily practice
of not second-guessing my beliefs;
to honor my personal integrity,
not give my power away to others.

☙

What Do You Have to Hope For?

Courage—unapologetic courage—
a quality we all possess to cover the gap
of what lies beneath. Courage
is acting against fear, to be in truth
in the midst of lies. I take courage like food,
allow myself to try regardless of outcome.

Without hope I would not have gotten through.
Hope is the seed of intention, helps me
think outside my constraints to build
something new on something old.
Hope is a beautiful field to a prisoner—
the places you find yourself can be exciting.
Hope is at the heart of every struggle;
struggling makes us appreciate it even more.

Without challenge I have no way
to know my own worth.
So try regardless of the outcome.
To be me is a sweet thing
no longer weak but a warrior.

Learn to Love

Proud and confident,
you're going to think you know it all;
there is no freedom if you see and hear
only what you want.

Break free the chains that keep you
from pursuing your dreams!
Ask one million questions.
Probe the subjects you fail to grasp
without fear. Don't give up—
sit and smile, bask in your questions;

learn to depend on yourself, to love yourself first;
then find a partner you trust who wants YOU
to thrive, authentic and compassionate.

Learn to love, and stick to it.

❧

Hoping to Fly

I hold myself here
tense, pensive and waiting.
The ones we love come and go,
ask for more memories on shelves.

My body screams
feeling like I'm looking down a rabbit hole:
try this, you may like it, savor it
a humming song begging for what I do not know.

Fighting no longer appeals.
I try to succeed but only fail,
the look of humiliation
more than I should for my age.

I am who I am, a failure in progress,
lost in words rather than flight.
The life within me gets quieter each day,
an unexpected direction.

Let life begin again;
laugh today like it would never end.
I would settle for friendship if only I knew how—
the place I started and the place I long to return.

❧

Beyond Reach

Sitting by the stilled pond slanted with light,
I belong to the earth, made from a grain of sand.
Behind those large honey-colored eyes
I grew to her melody awaiting my first
tender bloom as malleable as the reflection.
She recalls how it feels to be needed,
watched herself grow through me
her body becoming the wings of my waist
strong and more courageous than you know.
She twists her hair back;
I press my hand up against the smooth glass
inscribe love upon our bodies
her own signature tenderness.
Does she see me yet?
I follow in the footsteps she taught me.
More and more I see her
taking me back to the roots of my wildness.

☙

Superpowers

You gave me your superpowers
squeezing out vital thoughts,
the money and power you gave
like 10 cups of coffee.
You continued to feed me
made a monster out of me
crawling on my knees, at your mercy
left me there to die.

Tap a vein of new thought
midwifing inspiration and hope;
remove from imaginary pedestals
the Olympic athlete of arts and letters.
Articulating voice and vision
let soul awareness pour forth
as if my Wonder Woman stance
might reduce your own shimmer.

I do not need your superpowers—
super powers that took life away
took every ounce of dignity.
Your reflection fades
with my new perception of life—
free and clean to live happily.

Every Day Feels Like a Birthday

Born to grow, to lay down my past
(don't look back!); born to learn
through the heartache to land on my feet
sealing a deal with my inner self
to be home for my birthday,
finger sifting through fine sand
scanning the horizon. No more darkness
for this bright-eyed, beautiful woman
but a whole new life for me.

Worries and problems fade away as the years go by;
lost parts of myself all together.
Let the day pass boundless within these walls.
I am not here at all,
but wearing a beautiful dress
in summer cottages full of life,
my wishes microscopic grains of sand.

☙

Dear Women

There is so much I want to tell you.

I'm scared, sad—everybody's screaming
so eager to push one another, emotional
about not receiving a letter. So many women
here without a residence—women who struggle
and survive, hard working, self-educated.

All my teenage years I always did everything wrong.
I am ashamed of my life, want you to be proud of me.
Sometimes I'm so mad at your negative ways
of respecting yourself. Why did you leave me behind
in this hell hole so careless in how we treat
each other? It seems my life is at a standstill,
not perfect like my sisters.

I can understand what makes us who we are
in this new unreal world. One little surge
and our words go dark!
Thank goodness for paper and pen
that you can hold in your hand and read.

I think about you—so frail, hooked to a machine.
How thankful I am for part of my life stored away
I can relive whenever I want:
you in the garden singing, loud laugh, ear to ear smile.
How much I admire your strength
respect you more as a woman and as a mother.
It will be different when I get home, I promise.
I will be there for you, overcome it and move forward
stronger, and thankful to know better.

Dear Women,
This blip in my life is soon to be over
Number 1 is—*I never want to do this again!*

Spring Cleaning

Beginning a new part of my life, I find things
that are hard to let go of. Spring cleaning
is kind of what I'm doing here in prison:
clean out the guilty feelings, all the ugly things
swept away—pain, gossip, fear—
lock that bad person away,
the person I don't want to be.
Start anew trying to take care of me,
clean slate, blank canvas, the courage
to move on a new path in my life.

Time to start anew and see what I can do.
The artist within will paint earth's awakening
soul deep in dirt and desire, hungry
to work through the layers.

I am not here alone, empty inside. I am
two different people but the same person
at the same time, anxious and very nervous.
I don't want to screw up.

You receive answers one puzzle piece at a time,
tidbits of insight and guidance. Can you finally trust
there is only love encircling, protecting, restricting?

Breathe that knowing into your soul
searching the darkness for a face
stretched thin—by what?
Come to me, my arms are open for you.
Come, my child, my love and peace be with you
prayerful, self-centered and grounded.
Release your soul; stay the path
of self-reflection, a coming home.
Above all be still,
be spacious.

Now What?

Feeling lost in a world I birthed,
I sit in silences. Nothing to say
no longer anyone to call.
I hear voices laughing;
my voice is paralyzed
alone, abandoned, and betrayed
an unspoken language.

What you have is simply the truth—
I'll be home soon, forgiven one more time.
Now what?
Daring myself to have faith,
emerging humility and responsibility
my new lifeline behind a closed door.

∽

All the Girls and Women We've Always Been

. . . trusting, open-hearted, fragile, strong
depressed, weak, beautiful follower;
independent, addict, loving mother
healthy playful, bitchy, social butterfly;
scared, learner, pushy, persistent;
helper, hands-on, verbal, caring
nosy, outdoors-woman, drama-starter
responsible, respectful
selfish, open-minded; quiet, loud,
wild child, experimenter;
wispy attention-needy child,
Goth, not wanting to be alone,
brash, un-socialized, playwright,
world explorer, disgruntled American;
innocent, Daddy's girl, popular
child of divorce, unloved, isolated,
hard worker, survivor, student, listener;
hiker, animal lover, college grad, healed;
lost, lonely, scared child, blossom;
naive young teen; too young
single mom; pistol-packing cocaine dealer;
private dancer, awkward goodie-goodie
cuddly, jealous, non-verbal, ugly,
sleeping, proud, accomplished, sorry . . .

Dreams soon became dim
doing truly stupid things in search of attention,
such cruelty and pain unexpected at times—
popular by day, frightened by night—
my five-year-old mind tried to climb up a tree,
dissipate my shame. What have I done
to deserve these beatings?

I learn to trust and open my heart, my mind
snuggling near the woodstove. I learn to love
mountains, help others when upset large eyes
blink kindness to me. I stand in the woods
in a white nightgown yearning to learn,

keep trying a fresh start, able to win.
Give me a chance to love and not give up
laugher that fills the room, warm and safe again.
There will be no DOC stopping me from being free.

∽

The Dark That Is Deep

This is not just a wall, but a labyrinth,
a prison made by the sensation of being lost.
It seemed I had secrets, didn't trust myself enough
to let anyone in. I don't want to remember this,
but we have no choice; I'm scared to death
to be alone a minute longer,
a tiny white curl of a fetal girl.

I will not waste my breath on lost causes;
a void within me has shattered my perception,
the center spread everywhere.
How could you have known?

I still want, still yearn for you to see who I truly am.
You sit alone, hungry for it; you still taste
the futility of your effort, the waste
of a lifetime; a lifeline needs to shift, was definitely
skewed, makes me want to run and hide,
the destination meaningless.

Slowly the shawl of shame and despair slips
the breath, the rage, the steadying hands—
do you see what I see? With your help, a woman
of self-worth and confidence in full moon glow.

Shadows fall knowing when to sway,
pry loose my vision clouded in the aftermath.

∽

Reclaiming My Own Worth

My heart, my DNA behind a cage made of bones
vigorously pumping a rhythm I cannot control;
my clever heart doesn't listen to my brain's
lifetime of stories to tell.

My "not good enough" inner voice is old, wrinkled
and craggy, self-doubt released by a cast
of thousands their shortcomings viewed en masse
with megaphone in hand.

I can be the depth of love
and the black hole of hopelessness
melting off hard and twisted edges
exposed and puny in the light.
You'll never figure out identities
I've polished and fabricated
that combust into fine dust.

I lost momentum not completing tasks and goals;
didn't belong and not smart enough
to wring out self-doubt.
Self-loathing drug addiction would suffocate me,
making a mockery of myself.
Now, I no longer let fear drive me,
have a different way of seeing. Leading feet-first,
I have huge mountains to climb.

༺༻

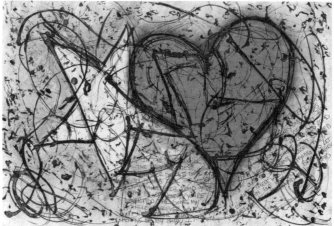

Artwork by Melissa G

Heart of Healing

Fears have imprisoned me looking for the bad boys
who won't give up on me drowning in high tide
half choking to death searching for a way back
to the light.

You have to get over the fear with God's help
and mine; quiet down and let air in the room
in times of need. Each mistake is a life lesson,
triggers a remembering pulling me up coughing
and sputtering. Having found the light,
mercy swoops down and bathes me in its aura,
polishes my heart for the better;
my self-inflicted prison lessens.

In whom can I confide? Is anyone out there
to fix my rotten choices?
Good is all I have, staying present.
I know there is a God. He will hear me;
healing will happen. Forgiveness comes from within
to free us from self-flagellation. Let the wafer dissolve
witnessing boundless compassion and acceptance,
God's saving grace.

I Am Waiting for Me

Some days I am emotionless
my heart waiting for me
to get rid of being scared,
to be carefree;

waiting for the months to pass
to embrace life in a new context,
bring truth from my past forward.
It's OK through my actions to change,

for love's gravity to pull me close to center
plant her foot firmly in my life.
My past may creep up on me
like a cocoon holding me prisoner to my addiction.
My truth is, it's time to let loose.

Awaiting the sunrise I take my first plunge,
take my first flight, feel like a butterfly for the first
time. Artistic memories of day's freedoms
lap waves of pink air at my toes.
There is a river now flowing very fast
giving flight to the whole world.

Beauty lies everywhere, even deep
within the heart of destruction.
Water meets stone—my world, my breath.
I desperately don't want to drown
but to create my own nest:
powerful, destructive, transformative healing
open to a relationship of tender heart
to fill oceans.

The truth within me is
I want to feel free of my past;
don't forget I have a rainbow over me,

an angel of freedom centered.
Together they become one.
I am bright and unexpected.
I will grow. I will shine. I will flourish.

＊

Survivor

In six years of empty time I've become a survivor,
forced to recreate myself,
bend and fold like a thin piece of paper—
but standing strong in my views and sensings
happy to be who and what I am
and not just for myself.

Gears grind, lead is shaved, smell of pine and cedar
the eloquence of days gone by. I feel it in my bones
now big and bold: *here I am—read me now!*
Say it loud and say it proud:
no more ripped out of the version of myself,
I write to heal; today, I live life, pause
as I gather composure running free,
to see the adult I was bound to be.

A yellow lead hexagon writes a person's measure
when voice doesn't tell all: energy and strength
to change for the better, build a new house, stay
out of trouble, free to be a missing piece of me—
a child of the divine—like swiping your hand over
silk. Love yourself; without a doubt the past
is dead and gone smudged out words
at the bottom of the line.

＊

Soul-journ

Behind me must be forgotten—addiction, the devil
critical of my hair untamed, unhinged;
Cupid's careless arrow plucked from the sky
swatting the air thick with trust, love, hope
and dreams vulnerable to the game;
thinking there's no danger is absurd.

The air was ripe with hate, uncontrolled emotions,
stagnating laughter that should thrive
stuck in a cage, angry screams embedded in cement,
voices that haunt me crawling through the under
brush of my life, the place nobody wants to be.

No matter how many mistakes I make
I can choose to laugh; be one of those birds;
heal with naked truth, dignity, and integrity;
pull my layers back so I'm tender.
Mouth wide open feeling the wind,
I have found courage and determination
boundaries I have set myself—
no angry looks or unkind words,
no drama. I have tunneled through torture,
have a strong sense of the absurd.

Nobody can stop me now. I long to live in this place
forever, lost in words, my own space
my internal conquest another chance for daylight
looking for me, this slightly cracked child of God
healing with intention more than sweet release.
That's what time demands.

It's a Lifelong Road

It's a lifelong road learning to love my flaws,
to be enough just as I am; longing
to perceive myself as others see me,
to understand my sickness, want my appearance
to match my personality; trying to learn to love
my life, not to believe in a life based on lies;
get better at loving myself—
look in the mirror and see my beauty,
force myself to love my ugliest truths.
Just because we aren't proud of some things
doesn't mean we can't be proud people.

I love *who* I am but not *how*:
my stick-like body and outrageous laugh
destroyed all my good moments; I'm hot-headed
a lot, rage my most comfortable emotion;
sometimes I'm so naive, I try to hide any way I can
the fear that kept silence. Inside, I never believed.
such an emptiness
forced me
to lie.

Feeling vulnerable is unacceptable.
I don't know what to do about
tender words of wisdom, sleek, gentle
and beautiful; a strong tribe of women,
sisters to walk beside me; my beautiful daughter
who came from me; possibility,
the one who stays.

All of a sudden I may be able to accept it:
not knowing I was doing it different,
didn't need to DO anything.
What a gift!

Starting Over

Good times become a memory,
dreams lost through selfishness.
I'm tired of living this life
waiting to be reborn in this stone-cold place—
overcoming shame, my wrongdoings;
tossed and tattered, I scream—but will anyone
listen? The size of sadness cuts back like a knife.

I'm lonely, scared, terrified. I've pleaded
and prayed for a way to make it right,
seeking things I don't deserve.
This life has molded me.

But good can come from nothing.

With a clean slate, I begin again,
validate these desires to start fresh
and start over, to better myself, tickle the soul
and warm the heart; to come and go as I please,
light candles in winter trees holding on
to the Divine, a good break to a bad end.

What am I waiting for?
Let me out into the snow
letting go of this life sentence;
let me walk out of here with a smile
breathing in each different season
guided from the stars.
Let the year shine.

◠

Ocean of Mercy

It is me, your daughter. I am here
come to terms with shadows that trail my heels,
wayward soldiers unbending in their demands,
my eternal shame chamber that shuts the door.

Lessons of introspection torn from the celestial
womb deeply embedded in all things beating
cleanse my soul, empower me to rise
from the bondage of my addiction,
making geometry of the air, unlocking my soul
to a journey of more.

In gratitude for what's in store
I wholeheartedly release
the smooth marble of all that existed.
Your grace has given me mercy.
I have become divine.

I exist, not stranded out at sea,
but linked into the collective.
The world opens its arms again
shimmering, flowing
an ocean of mercy
of new life, new encounters
by your star-swept hand.

Our Writing Container

We are all labeled from broken homes
and messed up choices, pitfalls spiraling
our lives out of order. Whose order?
Roads we took were thick with dust, unopened eyes
never truly knowing on the inside—
and you see the deed, not me.
Do you really listen?
take time to feed it, feel it?

I am where I am, changed.
It's unbelievable what we can find:
sometimes the light reaches down,
all perfectly aligned, the insides of me
envisioning a way forward
struggling with moods,
the oscillations of my life.

Here, we create community
permission, each voice unique
highly inspiring; we write
together, with respect and emotion;
share goals, let it go;
let some of me come out,
the looking glass a safe secure forum.
No one judges us or our writing:
we create words with meaning,
confidentiality, sincerity, an open mind
and a big imagination.

I have grown in my writing,
what I know my saving grace
grinding down and reshaping
boundaries, allowing me to unfold
what world I choose to live in.

About the Editors

By Allison Lowry

Marybeth Christie Redmond has long felt called to be a "voice for the voiceless." This inner compulsion to be in hopeful relationship with people who are outcasts or marginalized in any way is etched deep within her being and springs from her progressive Catholic faith. It is why, as a writer-journalist for more than twenty-five years, she has opted to cover stories that advance the dignity of people over "fluff" or high-profile news. Her own life journey has brought her to an evolving understanding that reconciliation is the core stuff of human life, while a lack of forgiveness in our own hearts and minds keeps us captive. This idea was furthered during a life-changing interview with Archbishop Desmond Tutu in 1986, as well as later travels throughout South Africa prior to apartheid's end. Marybeth's interests in incarceration and reentry were sparked by her friendship with a man imprisoned for more than twenty-three years for murder. She and husband, Mark, advocated for this man's release after he was denied parole five times despite impeccable behavior. The day he walked through the New York State prison gates to freedom was one of the more spiritually transforming experiences of her life.

In addition to co-founding and co-directing *writinginsideVT* Marybeth also serves as a regular commentator for Vermont Public Radio. She briefly served as executive director of Dismas of Vermont, a nonprofit organization providing transitional housing to men and women leaving the state's prisons. Upon relocating to Vermont in 2003 (as a lifelong New Yorker), she taught in the journalism department at St. Michael's College, Colchester, Vermont, for six years. She also served as media relations director for the Maryknoll Missioners, a global nonprofit organization of religious and lay persons serving in thirty-two developing countries. She has reported for TV news stations in New York, Connecticut, and Indiana, as well as writing enterprising stories about developing world issues throughout Latin America. Marybeth holds a bachelor's degree from the University of Notre Dame and a master's from the Columbia Graduate School of Journalism in New York City.

Courtesy of Jim Hester

Sarah W. Bartlett's deepest values were shaped from childhood by her father, a world-class chemist devoted to making the world a better place. A man of integrity and humility, he created an international professional community; personally, they shared a love of words at play.

A Cornell University Russian major, Sarah spent the first twenty-five years of her professional life using language in service to planning, marketing, and public relations for nonprofit organizations; meanwhile she continued her avocational calling to work with underserved populations that started with Head Start in high school. Yet her personal voice remained silent. Although she wrote constantly, she kept her writing to herself—until 1993, when she first participated in *Women Writing for (a) Change*. There she quickly embraced the life-altering power of sharing story within a mirroring community of women. By 2004 she had become trained to midwife new communities of women finding or reclaiming their voice and founded *Women Writing for (a) Change—Vermont, LLC*. In classes, workshops, retreats, and summer camps, participants use writing for personal growth and healing. Whether battered women, cancer survivors, mental health clients, adolescent girls, retirees, or the incarcerated, each writing community is co-created through the same intentional practices used in *writinginsideVT.*

Sarah's current work as change agent, mediator, and poet draws on the full range of her experience and prior training, including a doctorate in health education from Harvard. Sarah's publications include contributions to respected academic and literary journals, highly acclaimed anthologies, and her first poetry chapbook, *Into the Great Blue: Meditations of Summer* (Finishing Line Press, 2011). But none is as heartfelt or humbling as the present collection.

Language remains the medium for her own creative expression and within the communities she creates to support individual growth and social change. She lives pen in hand, eye and heart open to the natural world. Like the hummingbird who has taught her to see deep into the heart of things, she seeks to awaken the soul to presence. These are her humble offerings of beauty, balance, and peace.

Index of Authors